PANDOLFINI'S CHESS COMPLETE

BY

Bruce Pandolfini

A FIRESIDE BOOK

Published by Simon & Schuster

New York   London   Toronto   Sydney   Tokyo   Singapore

FIRESIDE
Simon & Schuster Building
Rockefeller Center
1230 Avenue of the Americas
New York, New York 10020

FIRESIDE and colophon are registered trademarks
of Simon & Schuster Inc.

Designed by Stanley S. Drate/Folio Graphics Co. Inc.
Manufactured in the United States of America

10 9 8 7 6 5 4 3 2 1

Library of Congress Cataloging-in-Publication Data

Pandolfini, Bruce.
    Pandolfini's chess complete : the most comprehensive guide to the
game, from history to strategy / by Bruce Pandolfini.
        p.   cm.
    "A Fireside book."
    ISBN 0-671-70186-X
    1. Chess—Miscellanea.   I. Title.
GV1445.P2579   1992
794.1—dc20   92-16152
                                                            CIP

ISBN: 0-671-70186-X

For Fred Reinfeld,
a chess writer
and Carmine Nigro,
a chess teacher

ACKNOWLEDGMENTS

I would like to thank Bruce Alberston, one of America's leading chess teachers, for his valuable input at all levels; Carol Ann Caronia for her constant advice and innovative suggestions on format; Idelle Pandolfini for her improvements on wording and presentation; Burt Hochberg for copyediting the manuscript; and my editor Kara Leverte, for her intelligence and inspiration, and for giving the whole thing life.

CONTENTS

9 STAR'S END 139

Endgame principles. Theoretical draws. Chief characteristics. Passed pawns. Pawn races. Square of the pawn. Turning maneuvers. The squeeze. Rook-pawn problems. Fortresses. Critical squares. The opposition: direct, distant, diagonal, rectangular. Corresponding squares. Extra minor pieces. Pieces vs. pawns. Opposite-color bishops. The active rook. Behind a passed pawn. Flank attacks. Cutoffs. Building a bridge. Checking distance. Philidor's draw. Queen centralization. The exchange.

10 SITUATIONAL PSYCHOLOGY 159

Blunders. *Luft.* Asking questions. Intuition. Move choice. Counting. Chess talent. Typical practical problems. Quantum chess. Playing the board. Keeping score. Best moves. Teaching techniques. Courses. Computer lessons. Analysis. Study programs. Opening repertoires. Where and whom to play.

11 COMBAT AND COMPETITION 172

Speed and blindfold chess. Odds games. Elo ratings. *Chess Life.* Touch move. *J'adoube.* Move completion. Scoring. Draws. Tie-breaking. 50-move rule. The clock. Time trouble. Grandmaster draws.

12 CHESSAMATICS 183

Compositions. Beauty. Art and science. Numbers and possible moves. Eight-queens problem. Diversions.

13 PUT IN PERSPECTIVE 188

Myths. Age and invention. Chataranga. First international tournament. World champions: oldest, youngest, winningest, and best. Prodigies. Grandmaster title. Hypermodern chess. Computers.

APPENDICES

INTRODUCTION

I have been teaching and writing about chess for two decades—that takes in three hundred days a year, answering about one hundred questions a day. In twenty years, I've probably been asked a quarter of a million chess questions.

Here, in *Pandolfini's Chess Complete*, arranged in thirteen thematic chapters, are 545 of them—answered. For the most part, these are the questions most often asked during my classes and private lessons, at tournaments and public presentations, and in correspondence.

Everything begins with moves and rules. Then come queries on tactics for mating and winning material; the application of opening, middlegame, and endgame principles; planning and grand strategizing; the use of psychological weaponry; methods for improvement and study; solutions to practical problems; teaching techniques; formats for tournaments and other competitions; chess history, personalities, and culture; and various unclassifiable questions about this and that—the raw stuff I've encountered in my work as a chess professional.

In selecting this material, I have aimed for straightforward instruction to clear up misconceptions, give fuller explanations of basic ideas often treated too briefly, and share the insights I've gained while helping thousands of students with actual problems over a score of years.

Yes, much of this is directed toward newcomers and casual players, yet there's plenty here for intermediate players, parents, teachers, students, and all chess enthusiasts. It's a straightforward text—rank beginners should have little trouble reading it, even without a chess set.

Pandolfini's Chess Complete covers a vast area, but it's not meant to be an encyclopedia. A few interesting questions might have slipped by, just as a number presented here may have eluded other chess teachers.

The level of the material generally proceeds from simpler to harder, but this is not a rigid rule. The same idea may be presented in several different chapters, depending on which aspect of it is being considered. For example, the concept of opposite-color bishops is discussed in both Chapter 4 (Material Evidence) and Chapter 9 (Star's End).

Use *Pandolfini's Chess Complete* any way you like. Read it right through if you're seeking logically organized instruction, or skip around as you might with a reference book.

If you are a rank beginner, turn to *Pandolfini's Chess Complete* as an introductory text, especially for an overview. As you move on in your play and studies, refer back here to clarify points you may find confusing in your later chess reading. It's mainly a book of advice, there for the asking.

SO YOU THINK YOU KNOW IT ALL

PIECES TO BOARD

1 □ **W**hat are the size and coloring of the standard chessboard?

The standard playing surface is a checkered board eighteen inches square. It is made up of sixty-four individual squares in eight rows of eight squares, each measuring two and a quarter inches per side. Slight variations are permitted in tournament play, but pocket sets are unacceptable. Many chessboards include a border of an inch to an inch and one-half on each side. Some borders contain letters and numbers to aid scorekeeping (as explained in the next chapter).

The squares of the chessboard are colored alternately light and dark, usually buff and green (or brown). The red and black squares common in checkers are almost never used for chess.

Boards can be made of thick paper or cardboard, but vinyl ones that can be rolled up and carried are preferred. Fancier boards, usually made of wood, are mainly given as gifts or used at home.

2 □ **D**oes the board have to be placed in a particular way?

The board should be positioned so that the players sit across from each other, with a light square in the rear corner at each player's right.

If I come upon a game in one of my classes where there is a dark square at each player's right, I make the students start the game over, even if one of them is about to checkmate the other.

3 □ **W**hat is a diagram?

A diagram is a pictorial representation of a position during a game, in which pieces and pawns are represented by figurine symbols. Unless otherwise indicated, the white forces start at the bottom of a diagram, pawns moving upward; the black forces start at the top, pawns moving downward.

Diagrams are usually seen in books, newspaper and magazine columns, and on scoresheets. Many diagrams have letters and numbers along the borders to help relate the position to a printed score. (Notation is addressed in the next chapter.) If there's a caption, it probably indicates the players and whose turn it is, and may also include the move number, what the previous move was, the name of the opening, and anything else of relevance.

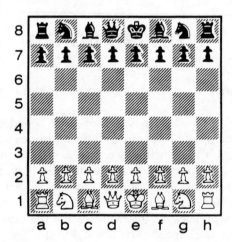

4 □ **H**ow many pieces are there in a chess set?

It depends on what is meant by the term "piece." If "piece" is understood in a general sense (any token or figure used as a counter or marker in board and table games), then a chess set has thirty-two pieces, sixteen per side, each white piece having a black counterpart.

But "piece" has a specific meaning in chess: it refers to any figure other than a pawn. A chess set thus has sixteen pieces and sixteen pawns, divided into two equal armies of eight pieces and eight pawns each.

To avoid confusion, I use the term "unit" to mean any chess figure: A chess set has thirty-two units, consisting of eight pieces and eight pawns per side.

5 □ **W**hat are the different kinds of chess units, and how many of each kind are there?

Armies are subdivided into eight pieces and eight pawns. The pawns are all alike, but the pieces are of five different types. There are two knights, two bishops, two rooks, one queen, and one king per side.

6 □ **C**an a game ever begin with fewer than thirty-two units (sixteen per side)?

There are two ways a game can start with fewer than thirty-two units. If it's not an official tournament game, the opponents may agree that one should have a handicap, called "giving odds." Typical handicaps are "rook odds" or "knight odds," where the odds-giver starts with only one rook or one knight; and "pawn odds," where one side begins with seven pawns and the other eight. Usually the player who gives odds plays White (because White always moves first), but when odds of "pawn and move" are given, the player who gives odds plays Black, allowing the other player also to have the first move.

Handicap games can also be arranged in tournaments specifically designed for that purpose. Such events are rare, not sanctioned by the U. S. Chess Federation, and not rated.

7 □ **W**hy can't I call a rook a castle?

You can, but it will mark you as uninformed. Although the rook often resembles the turret of a medieval fortress, in some chess sets it doesn't look anything like a tower. Even when it does, players never call it a castle anyway. It's like calling a knight a horse, which also won't win many chess friends.

Calling a rook a castle has the additional drawback of confusing it with the move of castling (see questions 73–87).

8 □ Chess sets come in myriad styles and sizes, but is there a standard version?

Since the late 1800s, the standard chess set has been the Staunton design. It's usually made of wood or plastic and the units are balanced so that they don't easily tip over. In some versions the units are weighted and the bases covered with felt. The king is normally approximately three and three-quarter inches high, with a base one and a half inches in diameter. The other pieces are proportional (see chart below).

White pieces are usually white, cream, or light tan. Black pieces are black or brown. A dull finish is considered best because it's easiest on the eyes.

SIZES OF STANDARD STAUNTON PIECES IN INCHES

Unit	Height	Base
King	3.75	1.5
Queen	3.5	1.5
Rook	2.5	1.5
Bishop	2.75	1.5
Knight	2.375	1.375
Pawn	1.875	1

9 □ What does the Staunton chess set look like?

In the Staunton model, the king is the tallest piece and is topped by a cross. The queen, almost as tall as the king, has a crown at the top. The rook is shaped like the turret of a medieval castle. The knight is a horse's head. The bishop is a slim, pointed piece with a diagonal slit on the top that suggests a mitre, the headdress worn by bishops and abbots. The pawns are the short ones. The six different kinds of units in a Staunton set are unmistakable. If you use a non-Staunton design, you're on your own.

10 □ How did the Staunton design become the standard?

The Staunton design was created around 1835 by Nathaniel Cook, who probably recalled earlier patterns he had seen. (Cook claimed that the motif for the knight was drawn from the Parthenon frieze in the British Museum.) He registered his design in March 1849, and six months later it was recommended in the *Illustrated London News* by Howard Staunton (1810–74), then considered the unofficial world champion. Although the patent expired three years later, Staunton allowed the phrase "genuine Staunton chessmen" to continue to be included with each set, which afforded some protection to the design. Ever since, this name, associated with Cook's design of chessmen, has become the accepted standard.

11 □ Is there any relationship between the size of the squares and the dimensions of the units?

The units should be neither too large nor too small for the board's squares. The standard proportion is that a square should be one and a half times the base of the king. As a rule of thumb, a rook laid on its side should almost fit inside a square, with a fraction to spare.

12 □ Can other types of chess sets, such as Florentine, Civil War, and onyx models, be used for play?

Manufacturers are at liberty to make any sort of chess set they think will sell. In offhand games, any set can be used if both players agree. But the greatest demand is for the Staunton set, which is used all over the world and is the only pattern accepted for tournament competition. Sets of other designs and nonstandard materials may be fun to look at and handle, but are poor for actual chess games because the pieces are unwieldy and not clearly differentiated. The real question is: Do you want a chess set for play or display?

13 □ Where are the chess units placed at the start of a game?

First, make sure the board is positioned properly, with a light square at each player's near right corner. The chess units are divided by color, White using all the lighter ones and Black using the darker. The units are set up only on the two closest horizontal rows (ranks).

The closest rank is for the pieces. Rooks go in the corners. Next to each rook is a knight, and next to each knight is a bishop. This leaves two vacant squares in the middle of each player's closest rank. White's king goes to the right one (a dark square) and the queen to the left one (a light square). For Black the placement of the king and

queen is reversed: the queen goes to Black's right (a dark square) and
the king to the left (a light square).

Each player's eight pawns are placed on the second rank, the row
in front of the pieces.

14 □ How can I remember where to place the kings and queens in the starting position?

If the board has been situated correctly at the outset, with each
player having a light square to the right, a simple rule applies. The
white queen is placed on the central light square of White's first row
and the black queen is placed on the central dark square of Black's
first row. A useful mnemonic for this is "queen on its own color."

2

AS NOTED BY
THE RANK
AND FILE

15 □ **W**hy do some chessboards have letters and numbers along the edge?

Letters and numbers on the borders of a chessboard are helpful reminders for keeping score. The letters are located under the files (vertical columns) and the numbers alongside the ranks (horizontal rows). Before starting play on such a board, set up the white pieces on the first and second numbered ranks and the black pieces on those numbered seven and eight. This is not compulsory, but otherwise the board is out of sync with the lettering and numbering, and it may be hard to record moves accurately. If you rely on these aids for keeping score, reversing the numbers can cause trouble.

16 □ **H**ow are the squares of the chessboard named?

Among the several methods used for naming the individual squares of the chessboard, the two most common are the algebraic and the

```
a8 b8 c8 d8 e8 f8 g8 h8
a7 b7 c7 d7 e7 f7 g7 h7
a6 b6 c6 d6 e6 f6 g6 h6
a5 b5 c5 d5 e5 f5 g5 h5
a4 b4 c4 d4 e4 f4 g4 h4
a3 b3 c3 d3 e3 f3 g3 h3
a2 b2 c2 d2 e2 f2 g2 h2
a1 b1 c1 d1 e1 f1 g1 h1
```

descriptive. In both systems, vertical and horizontal coordinates are combined to designate a square. Both systems are easy to learn and to use.

Other naming methods are possible. In the Udemann telecommunications code, each square is designated by two capital letters. In the Italian system used in the fifteenth century, each square is numbered from one to sixty-four. But the algebraic and descriptive systems are easiest to visualize and are consequently the most popular.

17 □ How are files named in algebraic notation?

Each of the eight files (vertical coordinates) is identified by a lower-case letter, from a to h. Starting at White's left, they are called the a-file, b-file, c-file, d-file, e-file, f-file, g-file, and h-file. From Black's perspective, the a-file is on the right and the h-file is on the left. The names of files never change; they are not subject to moves, perspectives, or shifting fortunes over the board.

18 □ How are ranks named in algebraic notation?

The ranks are horizontal coordinates. Each of the eight ranks is numbered from 1 through 8. From White's position (at the bottom of a chess diagram), the first rank is the closest, and the eighth rank is the most distant. Since the ranks and files are named from White's perspective, Black's home rank is the eighth rank and the rank furthest away is the first rank. These numbers never change, regardless of the game's circumstances.

19 ☐ **H**ow are vertical and horizontal coordinates combined to name squares in algebraic notation?

The vertical coordinates (files) are designated by lower-case letters (a–h from White's left to right), and horizontal coordinates (ranks) are numbered one through eight from White's side toward Black's.

To name a square, simply combine the two designations, starting with the letter. Thus, the dark square in White's left-hand corner is a1, the square above that is a2, the square where White's queen-knight starts is b1, and the square where Black's king starts is e8. But don't say or write 8e or E8; the letter always comes first, and capital letters are not used in algebraic chess notation.

A nice point about algebraic is that each square has only one name and the board has only one perspective (White's), so an algebraic square name is never ambiguous.

20 ☐ **H**ow can I determine mentally whether a particular square on an unseen chessboard is light or dark?

You have to know two things: (1) the "light-on-the-right rule," meaning that the board must be placed so that the corner square at each player's right is light in color; and (2) the rank number of the unseen square.

By applying the "light-on-the-right rule," you can easily determine the color of any other square along White's first rank (and Black's first rank, for that matter). Since the first square on the h-file is light, the first square on the a-file must be dark. The first squares on the other files, from White's left to right, must be: b-file, light; c-file, dark; d-file, light; e-file, dark; f-file, light; and g-file, dark.

The second step of the calculation is to imagine "looking up" the board. All the squares on a file that are on odd-numbered ranks (the first, third, fifth, and seventh) must be of the same color; those on even-numbered ranks must be the other color.

21 ☐ **W**hat is the difference between the kingside and the queenside?

The kingside is the half of the board on which the kings start. For White, it's the right half; for Black, it's the left half. It consists of four files, the e-, f-, g-, and h-files. Because the kings begin on the kingside and often remain on the kingside even after castling, most mating attacks are kindled in this half of the board.

Conversely, the queenside is made up of the four files at White's left and Black's right: the a-, b-, c-, and d-files. Both queens begin the game on the queenside.

22 □ How are the pieces named in the descriptive system?

The board can be divided in half in two ways: horizontally, by the frontier line across the middle, and vertically, by an imaginary line separating the kingside from the queenside. At the start of the game, the pieces at White's right (Black's left) of the imagined vertical line are called kingside pieces, while those to White's left (Black's right) are queenside pieces. The prefixes king- and queen- are added to the name of a piece to identify the side of the board on which it began.

In the original position, going from White's left to right, the pieces are the queen-rook, queen-knight, queen-bishop, queen, king, king-bishop, king-knight, and king-rook. For Black, the queen-rook begins on the right and the king-rook on the left. Notice that the black and white pieces occupying the same files at the start have the same names: White's king-rook opposes Black's king-rook, White's king-knight occupies the same file as Black's king-knight, and so on. The names of these pieces do not change, regardless of where they move in the game. The king-bishop remains the king-bishop even when it moves to the queenside.

Pawns derive their names from the files they occupy at any given time (review the next question on naming files descriptively). Thus, a king-rook pawn becomes a king-knight pawn by capturing on the king-knight file.

23 □ How are the files named in descriptive notation?

Files are the vertical coordinates and take their names from the starting positions of the pieces. The file (on White's extreme left) on which both the white and black queen-rooks begin is the queen-rook file. Continuing toward the right, there are the queen-knight file, queen-bishop file, queen file, king file, king-bishop file, king-knight file, and king-rook file. The names of these files remain the same regardless of where the pieces originally occupying them move.

24 □ How are ranks named in descriptive notation?

In descriptive, ranks are horizontal coordinates and are numbered one through eight, as they are in algebraic. But although in algebraic there is only one perspective (White's), in descriptive there are two, White's and Black's. Accordingly, each rank in descriptive notation has two names, depending on which perspective is being used. White's first rank is Black's eighth, White's second is Black's seventh, White's third is Black's sixth, and so on.

When using descriptive notation, if it's Black's move, or if you're discussing Black's possibilities, use Black's perspective. If it's White's move, or if White's position is under consideration, use White's.

25 □ How are squares named in descriptive notation?

As in algebraic, the vertical coordinate (the file name) is combined with the horizontal (the rank number). From White's viewpoint, the square on the king-bishop file that intersects the fifth rank is called king-bishop-five, or KB5 (in algebraic this is f5).

In descriptive, each square has two names based on perspective (see the previous answer). From Black's perspective, White's king-bishop-five is king-bishop-four. It depends on who makes the move. If White moves a piece to that square, it's KB5. If Black does, it's KB4. (When using algebraic, the square is f5 regardless who moves there.)

Descriptive notation is sometimes used in English- and Spanish-speaking countries, although it is in decline. In English descriptive, the file name is given first, followed by the rank number. In Spanish descriptive, the rank number precedes the file name. Both countries also use algebraic notation, however, which is more popular.

26 □ What symbols are used to abbreviate the names of units?

The names of pieces are often abbreviated, using capital letters: K for king; Q for queen; R for rook; B for bishop; and, to avoid confusion with the symbol for king, N for knight (some books still use the older Kt). These symbols are standard in both algebraic and descriptive notations.

Pawns are another matter. In descriptive notation, P signifies pawn, but in algebraic no symbol is used to designate a pawn. If a move is given in algebraic without indicating the unit, it must be a pawn.

Another difference between the two systems concerns kingside/queenside distinctions. In descriptive, it's often necessary to identify a move by using a prefix. If either of White's bishops can move to a bishop-four square, you differentiate the move by indicating whether it's the king-bishop (abbreviated KB) or the queen-bishop (QB). Another way is to refer to the square of destination, here a bishop-four square. This nomenclature also makes use of kingside/queenside distinctions (QB4 for queen-bishop-four or KB4 for king-bishop-four).

Some chess publishers use figurine notation, in which a miniature picture of the unit replaces the symbol. To my knowledge, U.S. Senior Master Karl Burger is the only person in the world to record his games this way.

27 □ What is required to record a move in long-form algebraic notation?

Long-form algebraic is full notation, including both the departure and arrival squares. (Short-form algebraic is just as accurate but offers less information; it leaves out the departure square and connective symbols, which can be useful to someone who is learning the notation system).

The long-form version includes: (1) the number of the move being played; (2) the symbol of the moving unit (a capital letter unless it's a pawn, in which case no symbol is used); (3) the algebraic name of the square of departure; (4) a hyphen connecting the departure square to the arrival square; and (5) the algebraic name of the arrival square. If the move is a capture, the hyphen is replaced by a lower-case x. Short-form algebraic uses neither of these connective symbols.

28 □ How are White's moves recorded in algebraic notation?

Consider the starting position. If White moves his kingside knight from g1 to f3, write 1. Ng1-f3. The 1. means that it's White's first move; N stands for the knight, the moving piece; g1 is the name of the departure square; the hyphen connects the departure square to the arrival square; and f3 is the name of the arrival square. (Note the period and space between the 1 and the N.)

In speaking, we would say "one, knight from g1 to f3." Or simply "knight from g1 to f3." In either case, we could drop "from" without any loss of meaning: "one, knight g1 to f3" or "knight g1 to f3." Some people make chess a second language and forget the first.

29 □ How is a capture recorded in algebraic notation?

You write it the way you would an ordinary move, except that the hyphen is replaced by a lower-case x (some people use a colon instead). Don't indicate what's being captured, only the square on which the capture takes place.

Suppose White's fourth move is the capture of a black pawn on d4 with a knight from f3. This move would be written 4. Nf3xd4. The 4. indicates it's White's fourth move; N means a knight does the moving; f3 is the square of departure; x means it's a capture, not just a move; and d4 is the name of the arrival square (the square on which the capture takes place).

No indication is given that a pawn is captured, only that something is captured on d4; this is just enough information for the reader to correctly play the move on the board. What more do you need than the names of the departure and arrival squares? You can see what's being captured, whether you're playing the move in one of your own games or replaying a game from a written record.

30 □ How are pawn moves and captures recorded in algebraic notation?

From the initial position, if White advances the pawn in front of the king two squares, it's written 1. e2-e4. If on the second move White captures a black pawn on d5, that is written 2. e4xd5. Note that no letter is used to designate a pawn.

31 □ In algebraic notation, does Black's recording of moves differ from White's?

Black's moves are written the same way, but with two slight differences. White's moves are written under White's column, and Black's are written under Black's. If a Black move is given with no White move preceding it, three dots or periods are inserted in place of the missing White move.

Consider the first move for both players. Suppose White advances the pawn in front of the king two squares and Black follows by making the same move. A completed first move would be written 1. e2-e4 e7-e5.

If Black's move is written independently of White's, however, it's like this: 1. . . . . e7-e5. The three extra dots replace White's move and indicate that it is Black's move.

32 □ Specifically, how does short-form algebraic notation differ from long-form?

We've seen (answer 27) that short-form algebraic notation omits the departure square. For example, if White's first move transfers the knight from g1 to f3, long-form algebraic notation would give it as 1. Ng1-f3, short-form as 1. Nf3.

In short-form, it's necessary to give more information only when two like units can move to the same square. To avoid ambiguity, you have to include either the file letter or the rank number of the departure square.

If two knights (one on g1 and one on e1) can move to f3, but the one on g1 does, write Ngf3 if using the short-form. If the one on e1 moves to f3, write Nef3. But suppose both knights that could move to f3 occupy the g-file. If the one on g1 moves to f3, write N1f3; if the one on g5 moves to f3, write N5f3.

There's no need to indicate a capture in the short-form. Obviously, whatever occupies the square you're moving to is captured. In the short-form, you give just enough to indicate the correct move, which usually means indicating only the arrival square.

33 □ How do you record a move in descriptive notation?

You should write: (1) the move number; (2) a capital letter (symbol of the moving or capturing unit); (3) a hyphen (means "moves to") or an "x" (means "captures"); and (4) the descriptive name of the arrival square. The next few questions illustrate descriptive's use.

34 □ How is White's first move recorded in descriptive notation?

Say White begins a game by moving the pawn in front of the king two squares ahead: write 1. P-K4. The 1. is the move number; P is the symbol for the moving unit (a pawn); the hyphen means "moves to"; and K4 is the name of the arrival square. The departure square is unnecessary. Finally, take note of the period and space following the move number.

35 □ In descriptive notation, if two like pieces can move to the same square or make a comparable move, how can they be distinguished?

As in short-form algebraic, sometimes a clarification is necessary to avoid ambiguity. The prefix Q or K can indicate that the moving unit is queenside or kingside. For example, you can differentiate between the king-knight and the queen-knight by writing KN or QN. To make matters even clearer, you can indicate the departure square by adding the rank's number to the piece's symbol (symbol first, number second). If, for example, White's rooks occupy K1 and K8, and the one on K8 moves to K4, write it as R8-K4 or R(8)-K4; if the other rook moves, write R1-K4 or R(1)-K4.

36 □ Are Black's moves recorded differently from White's in descriptive notation?

The main difference is that Black uses Black's perspective, not White's. Sometimes it's confusing because different moves can be written the same way. Should each side start the game by moving the pawn in front of the king two squares, both moves are written P-K4.

On White's turn, both sides keep score from White's perspective; on Black's, both sides keep score from Black's. When recording moves, both sides use the perspective of the moving side.

Finally, as in algebraic notation, White's moves are written under White's column and Black's under Black's. But if a Black move appears independently, with no White move in front of it, three dots replace the White move.

37 □ What is computer notation?

Computer notation is a version of long-form algebraic used in many chess computers. To enter a move, you indicate only the squares of departure and arrival, nothing else. There's no need to refer to the moving unit, since the computer knows what it is. Unlike other algebraic versions, either capital or lower-case letters can be entered, for the computer views them as equivalent. In fact, on many computer printouts, the moves are given in capital letters.

Suppose, White starts the game by moving the knight on g1 to f3. You would enter g1f3, which the computer would print out g1-f3.

WRITE IT DOWN

38 □ If White begins a game by moving the pawn in front of the queen two squares, how is that written in the four prevalent notations?

In descriptive, it's 1. P-Q4; in algebraic, 1. d2-d4; in short-form algebraic, 1. d4; and in computerese, 1. D2-D4 or 1. d2-d4.

39 □ **I**f on the first move Black responds by developing the knight on g8 to f6, how is that written in the same four notations?

In descriptive notation, it's 1. . . . N-KB3; in algebraic, 1. . . . Ng8-f6; in short-form algebraic, 1. . . . Nf6; and in computerese, 1. . . . G8-F6 or 1. . . . g8-f6.

40 □ **A**re the unit symbols identical all over the world, or do they vary from country to country?

Figurine symbols are the same worldwide, but letter abbreviations vary because each language has different names for the units. For example, the bishop's symbol in English is B, but in German it's L for "laufer"; and in Spanish the bishop is represented by A for "alfil." As for spoken language, none has universal acceptance in chess circles.

41 □ **W**hen recording a chess game during actual play, do players record only their own moves or those of both sides?

A player must record the moves for both sides. This is best done as each move is made. If you wait a few turns and then try to record a group of moves, you could forget some of them or their correct order. After White's turn, both sides should write down White's move under White's column on the scoresheet; and after Black's turn, both players should record Black's move in Black's column.

42 □ **W**hen you record a chess game, where do you write White's moves and where Black's?

Chess scoresheets use a columnar format, organizing the information in three columns. The first column on the left is for the move number (which is usually printed in advance), the second column is for White's moves, and the third column is for Black's. Both players write White's move under White's column and Black's move under Black's.

White and Black moves of the same move number appear on the same line. Each succeeding move appears on the line immediately below. Often the scoresheet is divided in half, with each half consisting of three columns. A typical scoresheet has room for sixty moves; the first thirty are written on the left, the second thirty on the right.

The columnar format is the standard and most convenient method of recording a chess game in progress. Should a game later be published, the score may appear in paragraph form instead of in columns, to save space.

43 □ Which is the best notational system, algebraic or descriptive?

When I first took up chess, descriptive was king and algebraic was "the other system." Today algebraic is dominant and descriptive seems headed for extinction. Some chess publishers prefer algebraic (especially the short form) because it takes up less space.

The current trend toward short-form algebraic isn't likely to change, so if you want to keep up with the latest chess literature you should get it down pat. On the other hand, if you want to be familiar with pre-1970 chess literature, including many of the game's classic texts, you should know descriptive notation as well.

For recording chess games, players tend to feel more at home with the system they first learned. For older players, it was descriptive; for youngsters and computer-oriented adults, it's algebraic. The most important thing about recording during actual play is to be comfortable. It shouldn't divert your thinking from the game at hand.

Every serious chessplayer should know both systems, but I recommend algebraic. Accurate, simple, and clear, its inner logic is more apparent and it even aids the learning process.

44 □ Why record chess games at all?

Here are some reasons for writing the moves down: (1) to settle disputes, particularly in tournament play; (2) to pace yourself and monitor your rate of play during a tournament or clock game, so you don't forfeit on time; (3) to reduce blundering by writing your moves down before you play them so you can check for potential mistakes and observe your opponent's reaction to your moves; (4) to enable others to learn and benefit from your efforts so that the game itself can evolve (this pertains especially to strong masters); (5) to look back on your own personal history to see how far you've come and what course your development has taken; (6) to become conversant with reading chess moves, so you can more easily study and improve; and (7) to show the games to someone (mainly a teacher), so you can learn from your errors.

3

MOVING WITH THE RULES

WHO'S ON FIRST?

45 □ How do my opponent and I decide who goes first?

No problem—the decision's been made for you. Whoever has the White pieces goes first. In checkers, Black starts the game and can make the first mistake!

46 □ How do we decide who gets White?

In tournaments, color allocation is governed by the rules of tournament chess and their particular interpretation by the tournament director. For example, in the first round, the higher-rated players may be assigned White on odd-numbered boards and Black on even-numbered boards, or vice versa. Color assignments are posted by the director on the pairing sheets for each round.

In offhand play you can choose for color informally. Hide a white pawn in one hand and a black pawn in the other. Your opponent selects a hand and gets whatever color is revealed. Another way is to flip a coin, the winner getting White. Whichever method is used, the players thereafter alternate colors from game to game, unless you can cozen your opponent into always giving you White.

47 □ Can a player ever make two moves in a row?

In a regular game, the players must alternate moves. The only exceptions occur in handicap games, often for stakes. In such cases, instead of giving a material advantage, the odds-giver may allow the opponent to take an extra move at an agreed time. But that isn't standard chess.

48 □ In a chess game, can I ever pass and not move?

The players move alternately. First White, then Black, then White, then Black, and so on. There are no exceptions. You can never skip a turn.

49 □ Can two units, friendly or hostile, ever occupy the same square at the same time?

It is illegal for two units to occupy the same square simultaneously. Nor can a unit ever be placed on the dividing lines between squares. Chess hustlers often try to confuse opponents into thinking a piece is on a neighboring square by moving close or partially over an intersection.

50 □ Must I move my king as a penalty if I make an illegal move?

There's no such rule. If you make an illegal move, you must retract it and try to play a legal one with the unit you touched. If there's no legal move with that unit, you can make any move of your choosing.

BACKWARD AND FORWARD

51 □ **W**hich pieces can move backward?

All pieces (kings, queens, rooks, bishops, and knights) can move backward. Only the pawns (which are not considered pieces) are restricted to moving forward. They move straight forward and capture diagonally ahead.

52 □ **H**ow many two-square pawn moves am I allowed to make in a game?

You may legally make as many as eight per side, which is one per pawn. But you rarely see a game in which all sixteen pawns negotiate two-square pawn moves.

53 □ **W**hich pieces can jump over other pieces?

Only the knight. As it makes its pirouetting "L-shaped" move to its destination square, the knight leaps over obstructions as if they didn't exist.

The rook is sometimes said to jump over the king in the act of castling, but in the castling move the rook actually moves around to the other side of the king.

54 □ **H**ow does a knight move look like the capital letter L?

If you trace the knight's move from its starting square to its ending square, the path resembles a capital L. To demonstrate this, add the starting square to the knight's two-one formula move. The long side of the L then includes three squares. If you move a knight from b3 to c1, for example, the squares b3, b2, and b1 form the long line of the L, while the squares b1 and c1 form the short part of the L.

55 □ **W**hen a knight jumps over another piece, does the knight capture the other piece?

No, the knight doesn't capture the units it jumps over. It captures only by removing the enemy unit that occupies the square to which it moves. The knight always makes a move of the same length, and in making that move it jumps over intervening enemy and friendly units. But none of those units, whether hostile or friendly (you can't take your own units anyway), are captured.

56 □ Don't I jump over a piece when I capture it?

No, you don't. When you capture an enemy unit, you move your capturing unit to the square it occupies and your capturing unit replaces it, removing it from the board. To capture by jumping is done in checkers, not chess.

KIDNAPPED

57 □ What is a capture?

A capture is a move that removes a unit from the board. A capture is made by transferring an attacking unit to a square occupied by an enemy unit. The move is completed when the enemy unit is removed from the board and replaced by the attacker. Captured units no longer take part in the game.

58 □ What is a recapture?

If your opponent captures one of your units and you take the capturing unit, you have recaptured. If you take one of your opponent's units and your opponent takes the capturing unit, your opponent has recaptured. The capture and recapture take place on the same square, often within seconds of each other.

59 □ What happens to captured units?

Captured units, which are dead for the rest of the game, are placed on the side of the board or otherwise off the playing area. The only way a captured piece can be revived is if a pawn is promoted. Otherwise, as an old Italian proverb puts it, "the king and pawns go back in the same box."

60 □ **W**hich units capture differently from the way they move?

Kings, queens, rooks, bishops, and knights capture the same way
they move, by replacing whatever occupies their destination square.
The pawn is the only unit that captures differently from the way it
moves. It moves one square straight ahead (except on its first move,
when it may advance two squares). But it captures diagonally, one
square ahead.

61 □ **I** was taught that chess pieces and pawns are called
chessmen or simply men. Why do you call them units?

I call them units because many men (and a few women) have expressed displeasure that so much sexist language is used in chess.
Some years ago I started using the word unit and now I hear fewer
complaints—about the language.

CHECKING OUT CHECK

62 □ **W**hat does it mean to be "in check"?

If you're in check, it's your turn and your king is under direct attack.
If it were your opponent's turn, your king would be in position to be
captured. When in check, you have no choice but to get your king out
of check somehow.

63 □ **H**ow do I get out of check?

Assuming one or more of these possibilities exist in the given position, you can: (1) move your king; (2) block the check by interposing
a friendly unit; or (3) capture the checking unit. If you have two or
more options, pick the one that helps your position the most.

64 □ **W**hat is checkmate?

Checkmate is a position in which the king is in direct attack (check)
from an enemy unit, and there's no way for the king to avoid capture
on the very next move. This means: (1) the king doesn't have a safe

move; (2) nothing can block the check; and (3) the checking unit cannot be captured. Checkmate ends the game without the king actually being captured.

65 □ If my opponent fails to get out of check, can I win by capturing the king?

If you attack the king without giving checkmate, and if your opponent doesn't see this check and plays an illegal move by not getting out of check, you still can't capture the king. It's illegal to respond to your opponent's illegal move.

The capture of a king is illegal, too, and must be retracted. The king has to be put back on the square it last occupied and a different move played.

66 □ Can a king move into a square adjacent to the enemy king, since "a king can't take a king?"

No, it's illegal. It's against the rules for a king to move to any square where it could be captured, regardless of the capturing unit. So, though the expression "a king can't take a king" is true, it misleads beginners to think a king is immune to capture by the opposing king and can freely move to an adjacent square.

67 □ Can any unit take any other unit?

Any unit can capture any other unit, assuming a legal move is played in the process. The only exception, of course, is the king, which can never actually be captured by anything.

68 □ Can any piece be in check?

Any piece can be threatened by any hostile piece, but only the king can be in check. Sometimes the word check is used casually to mean a direct threat to capture, but technically the term designates only attacks to the king.

When your pieces are menaced, you can guard them, move them, trade them, even lose them. But if your king is in check, get out of check or resign.

69 □ Can't a queen be in check?

A queen can come under direct attack from any unit (except the enemy king, which can't attack your queen because it would have to move into check). But even if directly attacked, the queen is not "in check," and you have the right to save it or lose it. Choose wisely.

70 □ Do I have to announce check to the enemy king?

Actually, there is no rule requiring check to be announced. It's not even considered courteous to do so, since the sudden announcement can jar the opponent's concentration.

Nevertheless, I often advise youngsters to announce check because of a novice's tendency to make illegal moves when the king is attacked. But on more advanced levels, announcing check is unproductive.

71 □ Must I announce a threat to my opponent's queen?

At one time it was considered a courtesy to say *"guardez"* when a queen was threatened with capture, but this is no longer done. Nor does declaring your plans for the enemy queen help your game!

72 □ If the kings can't be checkmated, is the game over when you capture the enemy queen?

You can win a game of chess: (1) by checkmate; (2) if your opponent runs out of time in a clock game; (3) if your opponent gives up; or (4) in rare cases, if the tournament director forfeits your opponent for violating the rules.

Capturing the enemy queen may make it easier to achieve a win but in itself doesn't end the game, unless it's also checkmate.

AT HOME WITH CASTLING

73 □ What is castling?

It's the transfer of the king and a rook, the only time during a game in which two friendly pieces can be moved on the same move.

If nothing occupies the squares between the king and one of the rooks (the one intended for castling), and if neither piece has yet moved in the game, you can castle by: (1) shifting the king two squares toward the rook; and (2) deploying the rook to the other side of the king, on the adjacent square. Either rook can take part in castling, though the queenside rook has a longer road to travel (one more square).

74 □ How many times may a player castle in the course of a game?

Each player may castle only once in a game.

75 □ When is castling illegal?

Castling is against the rules when: (1) any of the squares between king and rook are occupied; or (2) the king or the castling rook has previously moved. But it may still be possible to castle if the king and the other rook haven't yet moved.

In addition, castling is temporarily impossible when: (3) the king is in check; (4) the king will be in check after castling; or (5) if in castling the king must pass over a square guarded by the enemy (also called "passing through check").

76 □ How can I remove the temporary restrictions on castling?

(1) If the king is in check, get it out of check without moving it (block or capture the enemy attacker).
(2) If the king will end up in check, block, capture, or drive away the enemy unit(s) guarding the king's destination square, freeing it from enemy attack.
(3) If the king must pass through check, put an end to the enemy's control of the intervening squares (by blocking, capturing, or driving away the enemy units responsible).
(4) If a friendly unit is in the way, move it.
(5) If an enemy unit is in the way, get rid of it without moving the king or castling rook.

If all this fails, try castling in the other direction.

77 □ **W**hat happens if I try to castle, touching my king, rook, or both, and then discover the move is illegal?

If the king has been touched, you must make a legal move with it. Or play a legal move with the rook, if it's the culprit. If both king and rook have been touched, you must move the first piece touched if you can. If no move is possible with the piece or pieces touched, you may play any legal move.

78 □ **I**s castling disallowed if I've been checked earlier?

The right to castle is not forfeited even if a king has been checked. As long as the king hasn't previously moved, castling is still legal. Therefore, if you've answered a previous check either by interposition or capture, and not by moving your king, you can still castle and do great things.

79 □ **I**f my king can't pass through check, can the rook that castles pass through check?

First of all, only a king can be in check. The concept doesn't apply to a rook, which can be threatened and taken. Therefore, in the act of castling, the rook is fair game and legally can pass over a square under enemy control.

This situation can only apply to queenside castling and the square queen-knight-one, which the king never touches or passes over while castling.

80 □ **I**s castling permitted if I move my king once and then move it back to its original square?

No, you can't castle once you've moved the king.

81 □ **C**an I castle with a rook that's moved once and then moved back to its original square?

The rook can't pull this either. The rules state clearly that neither the king nor the castling rook may have previously moved in the game. It doesn't matter if they wind up on their original squares after moving away and back. Fortunately, you start the game with two rooks, and if you haven't done something with the other one, you might be able to castle the other way.

82 □ What is the difference between castling short and castling long?

Castling on the kingside is commonly referred to as castling short, while castling queenside is called castling long. The king always moves two squares, whether castling long or short, but the distance covered by the rook differs. For kingside castling, the rook travels two squares; for queenside castling, three squares. There's a difference in recording as well. For kingside castling the notation, in both algebraic and descriptive, is "0-0"; for queenside castling it is "0-0-0."

83 □ Can I castle with my queen?

Castling in chess pertains only to king and rook. The queen's only role in castling is to get out of the way to permit castling long.

84 □ Do I have to castle?

Castling is usually desirable, but it's optional. The only mandatory requirements in chess are to move when it's your turn and to get your king out of check.

85 □ Can I castle and give check to the enemy king with the same move?

Castling is usually a defensive move to get the king to safety. But it can also be offensive, since it activates a rook. There's no legal reason the rook can't give check—or even checkmate—as part of the castling move.

86 □ Does it make any difference which piece I move first in castling?

You can start with either piece, although it's customary to touch the king first and then the rook. At one time the rules mandated moving the king before the rook. Moving the rook first was construed as a rook move and you weren't allowed to castle. Today the rules are more understanding, though some opponents aren't.

87 □ Can I castle and capture on the same move?

No. You capture by replacing an enemy unit with your own. When you castle, the king and rook move across unoccupied intervening squares. It's against the rules to castle if any of these squares are occupied.

PAWN POWER

88 □ What is an *en passant* capture?

En passant (French for "in passing") refers to a special kind of pawn capture whereby a pawn on its fifth rank can capture an adjacent enemy pawn that tries to bypass it by advancing two squares.

The attacking pawn moves diagonally one square forward to the square behind the enemy pawn. The attacking pawn now stands on its sixth rank, on the same file as the enemy pawn. The capture is completed by removing the enemy pawn from the board. It is captured just as if it had advanced only one square instead of two.

Four conditions are necessary for an *en passant* capture: (1) the attacking pawn must be on its fifth rank; (2) the opposing pawn must have just made its first move, from its second rank to its fourth, so that both pawns occupy the same rank; (3) the two pawns must stand on adjacent files; and (4) the capture must occur on the attacker's immediate next move.

89 □ Are *en passant* captures compulsory?

Capturing *en passant* is a matter of choice, like any other move in chess. The only time a move *must* be played is when it's the only legal move. An *en passant* capture is not necessarily desirable just because it's available. As with any move, it should be justified by the position on the board.

90 □ How many moves can I wait before capturing *en passant?*

You can't wait. If you don't exercise the *en passant* capture on your first opportunity, you lose the right to capture that particular pawn *en passant*. However, you can capture other pawns *en passant* later in the game if the opportunity arises.

91 □ If my opponent agrees, can we ignore *en passant?*

Assuming both players are unclear about the *en passant* rule (and it's not a tournament game), it's simpler just to forget about it for the time being. For future encounters, look up the rule and use it.

However, if one of the players knows the rule it's not right to suspend it. The same applies to all the rules of chess. Players are not at liberty to ignore a rule they simply don't like. Nor can they invent their own rules. If you find this too stringent or too logical, try backgammon or a nice card game. The play is less rigorous and there's always the element of chance.

92 □ What is promotion?

It's the upgrading of a pawn into a piece. You promote a pawn when you finally move it to its last rank. At that point it may be changed into either a queen, a rook, a bishop, or a knight (but not a king) of the same color.

93 □ Can pieces be promoted as well as pawns?

Promotion applies only to pawns. A knight, for example, cannot be promoted into a queen. Lucky for pawns, unlucky for pieces.

94 □ What is underpromotion?

Since the queen is the most powerful piece, you usually promote a pawn to a queen. Changing a pawn into a knight, a bishop, or a rook is called underpromotion because each of these three pieces is less valuable than the queen. But in some situations, a new queen is not as useful as some other piece.

95 □ Is there a difference between "promoting" a pawn and "queening" a pawn?

There's no practical difference, because most promotions result in new queens. "Promoting" and "queening" are often used interchangeably, but while "queening" a pawn always means "promoting" a pawn, the reverse isn't necessarily true. You can promote without making a queen. Remember this the next time you need a knight.

96 □ Must a pawn be promoted upon reaching the other side of the board?

Pawn promotion is compulsory once a pawn moves to its eighth rank. You can't just let the pawn sit on the back row. It must be changed into either a queen, a rook, a bishop, or a knight.

97 □ Can I promote if none of my pieces have been captured?

Promoting a pawn is not dependent on previous captures. Even if none of your pieces have been taken, you can still promote to an extra queen or whatever other piece you need at the time.

98 □ How is a promoted piece different from a natural one?

Nothing distinguishes a promoted piece from a natural piece. They have exactly the same powers and limitations. They even look alike.

99 □ Suppose my pawn reaches the last rank and I want to promote it to a queen. If my own queen is still on the board, how can I actually replace the pawn with another queen?

You can borrow a queen from another chess set nearby. Otherwise, you can wrap a rubber band or a piece of tape around the promoted pawn to distinguish it from a regular pawn.

An alternative is to take a captured rook (if there is one) and turn it upside down. Most rooks are flat on top and can stand on their heads.

100 □ How many times can I promote in a game?

You can promote once for every one of your pawns that reaches the last rank—eight times, because you start with eight pawns. You can, in fact, have as many as nine queens (one natural queen and eight promoted ones), but the likelihood of this happening is very slim.

The most promotions I've ever seen in an actual game between masters is four: two for each side, with four queens on the board at the same time! Former world champion Alexander Alekhine (1927–35 and 1937–46) published a game known as the "five queens game," in which he had three queens (two by promotion) and his opponent had two (one by promotion). But experts now consider this game to be spurious. There are composed problems in which more promotions occur, but these were not actually played games.

I generally discourage students from queening too many times in a game, especially if they have an overwhelming position and don't need to make additional promotions. It's better to checkmate with one extra queen than stalemate with two.

101 □ Can I promote by capture and give check at the same time?

In the process of promoting, you can capture, give check, even give checkmate. There are no limitations or restrictions in this regard. If you perform several functions with one move, all the better.

102 □ Is it true that after promotion I have a one-move grace period in which my queen (or whatever) can't be captured?

There is no grace period for a promoted unit. If you promote a pawn, the enemy has open season on it for any capture or insidious attack.

103 □ As I promote to a new piece, am I allowed to place it back on its starting square?

Never. All new pieces start from the square of promotion.

104 □ Does promotion count as two moves?

Promotion counts as only one move. Though promoting a pawn seems to constitute two moves—the advance of the pawn to the eighth rank and its replacement by a more valuable unit—the advance and replacement are parts of the same move, just as the king and rook movements during castling are steps in a single transaction.

105 □ When is promotion completed?

The act of promotion is fulfilled when the pawn has been removed from the board and the player's hand has released the new piece after placing it on the promotion square. If the player has released the pawn but not yet touched its replacement piece, the move is not yet completed, though the player no longer has the right to move the pawn to another square.

SKETCHING DRAWS

106 □ What is a draw?

A chess game can end with either of two results: someone wins (and the other player loses) or neither player wins (or loses). The latter is a draw. In a tournament, each player involved in a draw gains a half point. An extra half point is sometimes enough to win a tournament!

107 □ What are the different ways a game can be drawn?

There are six ways to draw a chess game: (1) when neither side has sufficient mating material; (2) when both players agree to draw; (3) when stalemate occurs; (4) when fifty moves have been played without a capture or a pawn move by either side; (5) when the same position occurs for the third time; and (6) when one player perpetually checks the enemy king.

108 □ What is meant by "insufficient mating material"?

You have insufficient mating material if you don't have enough material to force checkmate, even with your opponent's cooperation. Obviously, if you have only a king left on the board, you can't set up checkmate even with Garry Kasparov's help, however badly your opponent plays. As soon as both sides have only a king left, the game is drawn. (Draws also result from endgames of king and minor piece vs. king.)

109 □ What is drawing by mutual agreement?

It means what it says: the players agree to split the point. One player proposes a draw and if the other player agrees the game is over. More than ninety-five percent of tournament draws are based on agreement, even though chessplayers are very contentious people.

110 □ How do you offer a draw in a tournament?

In order to offer a draw correctly in a tournament, you should: (1) make your move on the board; (2) ask your opponent if he will accept a draw; and (3) press your clock. The draw offer is then considered on the opponent's own time.

111 □ What are the most common ways to accept a draw offer?

Typically, there are three ways to accept a draw proposal. You can: (1) verbally agree; (2) offer to shake hands; or (3) stop the clocks. Any other method will do so long as your meaning is clear. (You can decline the draw by verbally disagreeing or by making your next move.)

112 □ I understand why a player with a losing position would propose a draw, but why would a possible winner accept?

A player with a superior position might agree to a draw not realizing that he or she has an advantage or how it leads to a win. The position could be so precarious that neither player wishes to risk defeat. In those instances, half a loaf seems better than none.

At other times, when the position is totally lifeless and with no realistic winning chances for either side, the players draw to conserve energy for later rounds in a tournament. But if you have any hope of winning, you should play on: nobody ever won a game by drawing.

113 □ Can I agree to a draw and then change my mind?

If your opponent offers a draw and you accept, the game is over. The draw is final and you can't change the result a moment later, even for all the pawns in a Staunton chess set.

114 □ What is a stalemate?

A stalemate is a situation in which one side, though not in check, has no legal move. In such a case, the game is drawn and the players split the point, no matter who is materially ahead at the time of the stalemate.

115 □ In a stalemate, why doesn't the side with a material advantage win?

The rules decree that a stalemate is a draw, regardless of material considerations. Actually, stalemates often occur when one side has a significant material superiority, such as an extra queen. If the stronger side isn't careful and moves in too closely with an extra queen, especially when facing a lone king, stalemate could result instead of checkmate.

As late as the seventeenth century, four different stalemate interpretations were in effect in Europe. Under Spanish rules, the side forcing the stalemate was considered the winner. In England the opposite was true: the side that was stalemated won. In France, the stalemated side merely lost a move and the game continued. But in Italy, which had the best chessplayers and where the Renaissance was in full bloom, the game was considered over and drawn. Since Italy had the greatest influence on European culture at the time, the Italian interpretation eventually prevailed. England was the last to accept the rule, at the end of the eighteenth century, with obvious repercussions.

116 □ Is it stalemate if on my turn my king doesn't have a legal move?

It's stalemate if you have no legal move with *any* unit. If your king has no safe square but you still have a pawn that can legally move, then the game is not a stalemate and play continues. I've seen many games where one player, unfamiliar with the rule's subtleties, gave in to the passionate demands for a draw ("Yeah, it looks like it") although a win was still possible and there were plenty of legal moves left with other pieces and pawns.

117 □ How can a game be drawn when the same position occurs three times?

A game is drawn when a player is about to play a move that would produce the same position for the third time, and that player claims a draw by announcing that fact before the move is played. If the move is played first, the draw cannot be claimed. The position would have to be repeated one more time before a draw could be claimed. The player must announce his or her intention before playing the final repetition.

A player may claim a draw only while on the move. Once a move is made on the board, action shifts to the opponent, and the player's right to claim a draw is lost for that move.

118 □ Can I claim a draw if I can play the same move three times, as long as I announce my intention before the third time?

Not quite. It's not that you must play the same move, but rather that the entire position must be repeated for the third time. Every unit, both friendly and enemy, must occupy the same squares each time the position is repeated. Moreover, all units must retain the same capabilities in each of the repetitions.

119 □ Do the repetitions have to occur on consecutive moves for threefold repetition?

To claim a draw by threefold repetition of position, you don't have to repeat the position consecutively. Any three identical repetitions are acceptable, whenever they occur, as long as: (1) the intention to repeat the position for the third time is announced beforehand; (2) all units are on the same squares and have the same powers; and (3) the same player is on the move.

120 □ In a situation in which I considered a threefold repetition, I could have castled early in the game, but although the position was repeated twice, I couldn't castle those times because the king had moved from its original square and then moved back. Could I have claimed a draw?

No. The threefold repetition claim doesn't hold unless every single detail is the same: the pieces must be on the same squares, the same player must be on the move, and the pieces must have the same powers they had when the position first occurred. If anything has changed, such as the ability to castle, the position is not the same and it's not a draw.

121 □ If the three repetitions don't occur on consecutive moves, how can I tell they've taken place?

When you're playing in a tournament and keeping score, the arbiter or tournament director can verify the claim by referring to your scoresheet. When you're playing an offhand game without keeping score, you're on your own. In that case, you better have an ace memory and be a persuasive talker.

122 □ Why would I want to claim a draw at all?

All players draw at times. It's better than losing. There are many reasons to claim a draw when the opportunity arises. You may be feeling ill or too tired to tackle the position. You'd want to claim a draw if your position were obviously a failure. You may choose to draw in a tournament because you're short of time or to insure your standing. A draw could lock up first place in a tight race. I'm sure you can add a few reasons of your own.

123 □ What is perpetual check?

Perpetual check is a way to draw by giving an endless series of checks. Mate can't be forced and the checks can't be averted. Perpetual check ultimately falls into the category of draws by threefold repetition of position, even though an actual threefold repetition doesn't necessarily occur. Once it becomes clear a player intends to check perpetually to force a draw, the players generally end the game right there.

124 □ What is the fifty-move rule?

It's the rule allowing a player to claim a draw if fifty moves have been played without a capture or a pawn move. If these conditions have been fulfilled, the player executing the fiftieth move can claim the draw immediately prior to playing the move.

125 □ Can my opponent claim a draw by the fifty-rule move on my turn?

You can only claim a draw by the fifty-move rule immediately prior to playing your fiftieth move (or your fifty-first, fifty-second, etc.), declaring your intention to draw the game. If you wait until your opponent's turn to speak up, then you lose the right to claim a draw until it's again your turn, assuming the possibility still exists, assuming you still exist.

126 □ Isn't it true there's also a twenty-one-move drawing rule?

No such rule exists. The confusion may stem from table tennis, volleyball, or the right to drink, where twenty-one can be significant. Similarly, there isn't a fifteen-move drawing rule, a sixteen-move draw, or anything else like the fifty-move rule. Trust me.

127 □ Can I claim a draw if forty-nine moves have been made and then on the fiftieth move a pawn is moved one square?

The rule states that once a piece has been captured or a pawn moved, the count must begin all over. So, if on move fifty a pawn is pushed or a unit captured, like Sisyphus you must start again.

4

MATERIAL EVIDENCE

TAKE IT EASY

128 □ Are captures generally desirable?

The answer to this question depends on the player's ability and the circumstances.

Experienced chessplayers base their moves and captures on the merits of the situation and nothing else. But beginners often don't know enough to be able to make such thoughtful decisions. Moreover, they're often reluctant to capture because they fear the recapture.

Some students repeatedly avoid winning capture sequences, balking at surrendering any material even when it's less than the opponent gives up. Some, for instance, will shy away from trading queens, even if it wins a rook. To overcome their reluctance, I may require these students to exchange pieces whenever it seems reasonable.

At the beginning level, there's another benefit to making many captures: the other side often forgets to recapture (or doesn't even see the possibility). The capturer then wins something for nothing.

129 □ Is it good to recapture?

You should recapture most of the time, or else your opponent gets something for nothing. Strive to keep a material balance. Pawn for pawn, knight for knight, knight for bishop, bishop for bishop, rook for rook, and queen for queen are typical recaptures.

There are three times, however, when you should delay recapture or possibly not recapture at all: (1) when taking back loses the game or leads to a lost position; (2) if you have a stronger or even a winning move; and (3) when you can interpose a useful in-between move (called a *zwischenzug*) before taking back.

Even so, after your opponent responds to your in-between move or moves, make sure you take back whatever you didn't recapture at first. If you don't, your intended victim could escape and you'll find yourself behind in material.

130 □ When I have a choice of recapturing with either of two pawns, why take toward the center instead of away from it?

Capturing toward the middle gives you more pawns in the center and a greater chance to control it. Thus the maxim: "Capture toward the center."

131 □ When is it desirable to capture away from the center?

Capture toward the center unless there is a good tactical reason to do otherwise or when your pieces need freedom to move through the middle without being blocked by pawns. Taking away from the center with the d7-pawn, for example: (1) clears the d-file for the queen and (2) opens a diagonal through the center for the queen-bishop.

Also, you might capture away from the center to avoid an isolated pawn. For instance, when you have the choice of capturing on c6 with the d-pawn or the b-pawn, capturing with the b-pawn isolates the neighboring a-pawn. Capturing with the d-pawn, on the other hand, keeps the queenside pawns massed in one unbroken group. Together is often better.

THE TEST OF TRUE VALUE

132 □ What is an exchange?

An exchange is a trade of equal value. It involves at least two moves, one for White and one for Black, and occurs when you capture an enemy unit and a different enemy unit captures back, regaining the material balance. You can exchange a pawn for a pawn, a minor piece for another minor piece, a rook for a rook, or a queen for a queen.

Another kind of exchange involves unlike units that are of comparable worth. Some examples are a knight for three pawns; a rook for a knight and two pawns; a bishop and a knight for a rook and two pawns; and a queen for a rook, a knight, and a pawn.

You can't say you've made an exchange, however, when you give up a queen and only get a rook in return. That's not exchanging material, that's losing it.

133 □ Can I lose time by exchanging?

You can lose time when: (1) you exchange a developed piece for an undeveloped one; (2) your opponent retakes with a developing move; and (3) your opponent retakes with an already developed piece while positioning it on a more effective square.

134 □ How can I gain time by exchanging?

An even exchange gains time when it forces your opponent to respond with a nondeveloping or useless move, so that the next useful move is still yours.

Say your opponent threatens to capture an unguarded knight with a knight. If you protect the knight, or move it to safety, your opponent retains freedom of choice. If instead you take the enemy knight, and your opponent recaptures to avoid material loss, your next move is "free." Or you can withdraw the knight, surrender the initiative, and practice defense.

135 □ What are the relative values of the pieces?

The material values of the pieces are based on their comparative worth in pawns. Bishops and knights are worth about three pawns each, rooks are worth about five pawns, and queens are worth about nine pawns. (The king has no exchange value because it can't legally be captured. In terms of attacking ability, however, it's probably worth about four pawns.)

Some books give slightly different values; for example, a queen is worth about ten pawns. But all books agree these values are relative and subject to variation in the context of specific situations.

An unstoppable pawn about to queen is more valuable than a distant knight, while an unobstructed bishop supporting a mating attack may outweigh a blocked-in rook with no open files. But in most cases the accepted values hold true.

136 □ **I**n the opening, it's often possible to exchange the king-bishop and the king-knight for the opponent's king-rook and king-bishop pawn. Which combination is preferable, the bishop and knight or the rook and pawn?

Two minor pieces are generally preferable to a rook and a pawn in the opening and middlegame (the balance of power shifts in the endgame). The bishop and knight begin to pull their weight almost from the moment they leave their home rank, making them particularly valuable in the early stages of a game. They become effective immediately for both attack and defense. The rook and pawn, on the other hand, aren't as readily deployed.

Rooks tend to have little impact in the opening. Even after castling they're often half asleep. Usually, rooks are at their best in the late middlegame and approaching endgame. By then, files are open and the board is sufficiently clear for the rook to strut its stuff. That's when the rook awakens for action. (In fact, in many endgames, a lone rook is just as strong as a knight and a bishop combined.)

As for the plodding pawn, its offensive scope is practically nil. It's essentially a defensive unit, best left at home on its original square until the endgame, when visions of promotion can aspire it to greatness.

137 □ **I**f it's true that minor pieces are worth three pawns each, why are a bishop and a knight together often considered equivalent to seven pawns, while a rook and a pawn are worth only six?

First of all, minor pieces are not worth *exactly* three pawns each. These are rounded-off values used for convenience. In most opening and middlegame cases (values change somewhat in the endgame), a knight is worth a smidgen more than three pawns, and a bishop is perhaps a fraction more valuable than that. Their real combined value is closer to six and a half pawns.

But two minor pieces working collaboratively gain in collective value, so the whole is greater than the sum of the parts. Consider just the mobility of a bishop and a knight compared with that of a rook and a pawn. A bishop and a knight can attack simultaneously thirty-two different squares, limited only by the bishop's inability to guard the opposite color. These squares can be on any of the eight files or ranks. On the other hand, a rook and a pawn together can attack simultaneously only twelve squares on only two files and six ranks, the pawn's horizon being extremely limited.

In the beginning stages (though not necessarily in the endgame), the bishop-and-knight combination clearly is a much more potent weapon than the rook-and-pawn, which gives us insight into why the minor pieces must be worth more than six pawns. Actually, prior to the endgame, it's not unreasonable to rate their cooperative value at seven pawns, or equal to a rook and two pawns.

138 □ If bishop-and-knight combos are so valuable, why are the king-bishop and king-knight so often sacrificed for the king-rook and king-bishop-pawn?

This "sacrifice" is often played because of two mistaken beliefs: (1) that the transaction is for equal value; and (2) that having captured on f7 (or f2), the defending king will be exposed to attack.

First, the transaction is not an equal one; a bishop-knight team usually is more valuable than a rook-pawn team (except in many endgames). Second, once the defending king recaptures the second minor piece, it's not necessarily subject to attack since the most likely attackers (the enemy king-bishop and king-knight) have already disappeared from the board. In many cases, after the sacrifice the defender is better developed, still having all the minor pieces with which to prevent the opposing forces from approaching and attacking the moved king. Moreover, the king can probably "recastle" by hand, simply retreating to its castling square.

The attacker, thinking nothing is lost while an attack is being built, actually drops about one pawn in material and fails to obtain sufficient play against the temporarily exposed king. It's usually a bad deal.

EXCHANGE PLACE

139 □ What does "winning the exchange" mean?

You win the exchange by trading a bishop or a knight for a rook, a net gain of about two pawns in value. You "lose the exchange" when you're on the short end of the same deal. (Instead of saying "winning the exchange" or "losing the exchange," some people say "winning quality" or "losing quality.")

If you're "up the exchange," your opponent must be "down the exchange." You can also "sacrifice the exchange," which means you voluntarily give up a rook for a minor piece, either for tactical or strategic considerations. But because the term "exchange" also means an even trade, it's important to realize when "the exchange" does *not* refer to even transactions.

140 □ When I'm up the exchange, how should I try to play for a win?

Being up the exchange means more in some situations than others, but it always refers to cases in which one side has gained a rook for a bishop or a knight. (I'm assuming that the other forces on the board balance out for White and Black, the only difference being the rook for the minor piece.)

Generally, to win in this situation you must head for the endgame, trading off pieces (but not necessarily pawns) and trying to create the pure situation of rook vs. minor piece, with no other pieces on the board (though with several pawns).

From there, position your rook actively, trying to tie down the enemy king and minor piece, forcing them into defensive positions. Meanwhile your own king should take an aggressive stance, moving to key points or attacking positions.

If this approach doesn't bring further material gain, you may be able to surrender the rook for the enemy minor piece, gaining an extra pawn in the process. You then win by promoting the pawn or using it as a decoy to gain more pawns elsewhere. Eventually, you win by promoting a pawn to a queen and subsequently forcing checkmate.

141 □ When behind by the exchange (with a minor piece against a rook), how should I play to increase my drawing chances?

Swapping pawns skillfully, you may be able to convert to an endgame with no pawns in which your lone minor piece confronts the enemy rook. With careful play that kind of endgame is usually drawn, for there are no pawns left and it's difficult to force checkmate or win the minor piece. But the draw isn't automatic; being up the exchange is obviously still a definite advantage.

142 □ How important is a material advantage?

When a game is over, count the units remaining on each side. Most of the time, the winner is stronger in material. Usually the larger army has a better chance to force checkmate.

Material advantage is the foundation of chess strategy. Whatever your plan, you are better able to enforce it with a larger, more potent army. Experienced players guide their play accordingly, developing quickly and looking for ways to win pieces and pawns. At the same time, they maintain a constant alertness to ward off and parry similar enemy threats to gain material. Eternal vigilance is the way.

143 □ How do I gain a material advantage?

One of the most difficult things in chess is to keep all your material. In the first dozen moves or so, your opponent is likely to place one or more units in position to be captured for nothing. Look for these desserts and gobble them.

If waiting for these oversights is too passive for you, you can take a more active stance. Use your pieces (not your pawns) to attack the opponent's undefended targets. Try to set up double attacks, threatening two or more enemy units simultaneously. If you keep up the pressure, issuing constant attacks, your opponent is eventually bound to miss a threat or two and you'll come away with material gain. This may seem simplistic, but it's exactly how most chess games go between average players. Just watch.

144 □ How do I gain material from strong players?

Most strong players know how to hang on to their material. They don't put units where they can be taken for nothing, and they can easily see through direct threats. To beat an opponent of this caliber, more complicated tactics are usually needed.

I recommend trying to set up double attacks, one of which is obvious, the other more subtle. This gives you a practical chance, because it's natural for a defender to see the obvious attack (such as a threatened checkmate) and miss the hidden danger (such as a threat to transfer to the other wing to fork two units). Even an experienced player might be hooked by a series of these lethal snares.

If this doesn't work, you'll have to try more advanced methods, outplaying your opponent positionally before reaping the harvest—like a grandmaster.

145 □ What do I do after I've gained an advantage in material?

Once you've obtained a material advantage, you should exchange pieces, thereby emphasizing your advantage while reducing the enemy's potential for counterplay. Exchanges weaken your opponent's capacity to resist. Your goal should be to eliminate all the opponent's pieces, forcing a pure pawn endgame. Try to trade queen for queen, rook for rook, and minor piece for minor piece. When trading minor pieces, aim to swap bishops for bishops and knights for knights, avoiding endings of knight versus bishop, or bishop versus knight, where your remaining minor piece may be less effective.

The trading-down policy doesn't pertain to pawns, however. Pawns are what you'd prefer to *win*. As you trade pieces, the defender's ability to guard the pawns decreases, and you might get them for nothing.

Moreover, exchanging too many pawns, particularly in minor-piece endings, could give your opponent surprising opportunities to draw. For example, the ending of minor piece and pawn versus minor piece is drawn if the defender sacrifices the piece for the pawn. After the sacrifice, the attacker does not have sufficient mating material.

Other foolish trades might allow the defender to set up an impregnable "fortress," in which passive defense holds. So, remember the maxim "When ahead, trade pieces, not pawns." If you do swap pieces, make sure they're the right ones.

146 □ What are the most serious dangers to a player who has gained a material advantage?

The dangers are psychological and positional, and, like Tweedledum and Tweedledee, they go together. It's natural for a player to relax or get complacent after gaining material, thinking the game's already won. But when the opponent resists, the win can easily slip away. Extra material doesn't guarantee a win. You still have to make it work for you.

In winning material, your forces could become separated from the main theater and unable to fight off enemy invaders. Be especially careful not to stretch your army to win a questionable pawn if it leaves certain key pieces (such as the queen) out of position for defense.

Try to avoid a psychological letdown and stay alert. Cope with disarray in your forces by: (1) consolidating; (2) warding off potential threats; (3) activating key forces; and (4) simplifying ruthlessly. Trade enough pieces and your opponent will have nothing left to do. But you still shouldn't relax—not until you get the point.

147 □ Why do many players resign when behind in material?

Some players resign when a material deficit implies a hopeless position. A clear case would be to fall behind by a queen against a master. Strong players can win these positions effortlessly. But it takes a certain level of sophistication to realize when a situation is futile.

If you're a beginner, however, resigning seldom makes sense, especially when your opponent is a beginner and probably has no idea how to exploit a winning material advantage. How do you acquire this expertise? By playing on even in lost positions and observing how stronger opponents crush you. Build up your skill by losing a lot, and eventually you can resign whenever you want.

148 □ In analyzing a position, how should I determine the material situation?

You count and compare material on the board, step by step. I recommend beginning with a pawn count, because if there's a disparity, it's likely to be reflected there.

While analyzing the material situation, don't think in terms of points. If you have a knight and your opponent has two pawns, don't say you are ahead by one point. Note precisely what the difference is, saying that you have a knight for two pawns. Formulating such comparisons, instead of adding points, tells you more about your advantage and aids in planning.

Start by counting the white pawns and then the black. Compare and note the difference, if any. Then move to the minor pieces, counting and comparing and noting whether they are knights or bishops. Then count and compare rooks, then queens. Throughout your analysis, keep a running comparison in your head so that you don't forget your earlier calculations. By always proceeding in the same order, you're less likely to overlook a type of unit and make a mistake.

MAKING A SACRIFICE

149 □ What is a sacrifice?

A sacrifice is the voluntary surrender of material to earn other advantages. You might sacrifice to gain time, maintain the initiative, build an attack, stop the other side from castling, expose the enemy king, or gain positional pluses that can't be given a concrete value. Sometimes a sacrifice is merely temporary, and the material is soon regained by force and with interest, the sacrificer coming out ahead.

A correct sacrifice should work against even the best defense. Unsound sacrifices can be refuted if the defender responds correctly. To make a sound sacrifice, first envision the consequences and be sure you like what you see before you give up material.

150 □ What is the most common kind of sacrifice?

A typical sacrifice is an opening gambit of a pawn. As a rule of thumb, if you gambit a pawn in the opening, aim to get ahead by three moves in development. You can tell whether such a sacrifice is sound by using these criteria: Does it (1) gain time and meaningfully augment development? (2) establish a powerful two-pawn center? (3) prevent the enemy from castling, either temporarily or permanently? (4) gain a strong attack or initiative? or (5) lure the enemy queen out of position?

151 □ Why are sacrifices so often misunderstood or under- rated?

For a sacrifice to be sound, the sacrificer's circumstances must improve at least slightly. But most players tend to overlook sacrifices that lead only to small gains, preferring instead to focus on the enemy king and the major pieces. Many opportunities are therefore never considered, or are rejected as trivial.

Another reason sacrificial possibilities are dismissed is that they may require too large an investment. Some competitors, for example, are unwilling to sacrifice their queen under any circumstances.

There are also players who don't fully understand that most winning sacrifices are not really sacrifices at all. Is it a sacrifice when you know that if it's accepted you will win by force? Wouldn't you give up your queen to win the game?

It's important to distinguish between real sacrifices and sham ones. A real sacrifice involves risk and its consequences are unclear. Most sham sacrifices, on the other hand, are merely preludes to winning combinations. No sacrifice, just smart chess.

152 □ If I can't conclusively analyze my opponent's offer of a sacrifice, what should I do?

When you can't decide why your opponent offers a sacrifice, accept it. If you can see that the sacrifice will work, of course don't risk taking it, but if you can't see any reason behind the offering, why not take the bait? Either you'll be right and will gain material because the sacrifice is unsound, or you'll be wrong and lose the game—but in that instance you'll learn something.

In any case, you'll hate yourself—and your opponent—if you miss the obvious.

A NATURAL SUPERIORITY

153 □ When is a bishop better than a knight?

A bishop is usually better when: (1) the position is open and diagonal attacks from far away are possible; (2) there are potential targets or operations on both sides of the board; (3) facing a knight, which the bishop can corral on the side of the board; and (4) time-gaining or time-losing moves must be played, when the same key squares remain guarded by the bishop after it moves. A knight can't move and still keep an eye on the same squares.

154 □ How can a bishop "lose a move"?

Although this sounds negative, it's actually a favorable tactic. A bishop loses a move by shifting along a diagonal it already occupies and controls. This stratagem, mainly applicable to the endgame, forces the opponent to move when it's undesirable to do so, leading to a concession. The essential aspects of the position remain unchanged. However, instead of it being your move, suddenly it's your opponent's. You lose a move but gain in position.

155 □ When is a knight preferable to a bishop?

Knights get the nod over bishops when: (1) the position is blocked and the knight can jump over obstructions that impede a bishop; (2) the knight is anchored deep in the enemy position and can't be dislodged; and (3) squares of both colors must be guarded. The last condition obviously can't be satisfied by a bishop, which can guard only the color it travels on.

156 □ What does it mean to "win the minor exchange?"

If you "win the minor exchange," you win a bishop for a knight. This is considered advantageous because in most positions bishops have the upper hand.

But be careful about playing for the minor exchange to the exclusion or omission of other factors. Make sure the resulting situation will actually favor your bishop over the enemy knight. Meanwhile, don't forget to secure your pawns, your king, and your position.

157 □ Why are two bishops generally superior to a bishop and a knight or to two knights?

Two bishops are stronger than other minor-piece combinations because, when working in harmony, they negate a single bishop's chief failing, the inability to guard squares of both colors. In cooperation, each bishop stands sentinel for the other, allowing each to achieve its full potential.

United bishops tend to be stronger than other minor-piece combinations because they: (1) control the center more easily, either aligned in the same direction or crosswise from opposite sides of the board; (2) are effective long-distance attackers and therefore don't have to be close to their targets, as do knights; (3) restrict minor-piece movement better, especially by corralling knights along the board's edge, preventing their safe movement; (4) induce pawn weaknesses with greater ease, whether from far away or behind the pawns; (5) more fluidly support an invasion by their own king and gain tempi to make it happen; (6) create favorable exchanges more readily, often enabling simplification to good-bishop-vs.-bad-minor-piece endgames; (7) contend satisfactorily with advancing pawn masses, for though driven away, bishops remain in attacking position by staying on the same diagonals, still assailing enemy pawns and the squares over which they must pass; and (8) convoy a passed pawn splendidly, controlling in concert consecutive diagonals before the advancing pawn, clearing a path to its promotion. Basically, two bishops are wonderful.

158 □ **W**hy do some players, most notably the immortal Samuel Reshevsky, prefer having a combination of bishop and knight to either two bishops or two knights?

A bishop-and-knight combination may be preferable when it's not clear where the position is going and whether the resulting situations will favor a knight or a bishop. By keeping one of each, you're covered for any possibility.

By being able to guard squares of both colors, the knight is suited for both offensive and defensive action. For example, it can attack squares of one color while occupying the other color, enabling it to confront an opposing bishop without the bishop being able to attack the knight. Moreover, by covering squares a friendly bishop can't cover, all squares can be influenced.

Style is another factor. Some players have a bent for manipulating the bishop-and-knight combination, but this only works when the position permits such flexibility.

159 □ **I**f bishops are generally superior to knights, why are a queen and a knight working together preferred to a queen and a bishop?

In either case, the real power is the queen and the various attacking motifs at its disposal. The bishop is an imperfect partner for the queen because at most it can only guard half the squares on the board, and only squares of one color at that. It can't protect a queen occupying a square of the other color.

A knight, however, is capable of attacking all of the board's squares and can offer the queen twice as many support points as the bishop. More important, the bishop merely duplicates the queen's diagonal move, but the knight moves in a way the queen can't, adding an extra dimension to the assault. If the knight can get near the target, it's an excellent attack-mate for the queen, both as a supporter and in its unique weaponry.

OPPOSITES ATTRACT

160 □ What does having bishops of opposite colors mean?

This means one player has a bishop traveling on light squares while the other has a bishop using dark squares. These bishops can never attack each other.

161 □ When is an opposite-color bishop desirable?

This bishop is particularly good in the endgame, especially if you happen to be in bad shape and are aiming for a draw by setting up a blockade on squares the enemy bishop can't control. It can also be a plus in the middlegame, when engaging in a general series of attacking moves. In that case, the enemy's bishop can't guard the squares attacked by your bishop. During the attack period, it's like having an extra, unopposed, aggressor.

162 □ In what ways are pawns different from pieces?

Pawns are radically different from the other chess units. They (1) capture differently from how they move (every other piece captures the way it moves), which enables an enemy unit to block their movement by occupying the square directly in front of them without fear of capture; (2) can never move backward, which means that once they abandon control of a square, they can never guard it again; (3) have very limited scope and cannot traverse the board freely like the pieces; (4) move more slowly than any other unit, which makes it essential to include them in long-range planning; (5) are the only units that can become something else (by promotion), which means their value is highly subject to the nature of the position and the phase of the game (their stock goes up in the endgame); (6) begin the game on their side's second rank (everything else starts on the front rank); (7) are the least valuable of all units, and so are used as the basic measure of value for the pieces; (8) are more numerous than any other unit; and (9) have possibilities contingent on special rules, such as the two-square option on each pawn's first move and *en passant* captures.

163 □ Which pieces are hampered the most by blocked pawn structures?

Bishops are usually most affected by constricted pawn formations. Traveling on squares of one color, a bishop at most can attack only half the board's squares, but if those squares are blocked by its own pawns or obstructed by secure enemy pawns, its mobility is even further reduced.

Queens, rooks, and kings may also suffer in blocked positions, but they often have alternatives denied to the bishop. If light-square diagonals are blocked, for example, the queen may still be able to shift to a dark square or move along ranks and files. Knights, on the other hand, may be at home in some blocked positions if the obstructions can be conveniently scaled.

164 □ How can a knight get from one light square to another light square?

A knight can get to the same color square in an even number of moves: two, four, six, and so on. This is because every time the knight makes its two-and-one formula movement it transfers to a different-color square. It goes from light to dark to light to dark.

165 □ How can a dark-square bishop influence a light square?

A bishop can influence squares different from the color it travels on by attacking, capturing, or threatening an enemy unit guarding other color squares. If a bishop, for example, menaces a knight occupying a light square, the bishop is really loosening the opponent's grip on the dark squares guarded by the knight. If that knight disappears or moves away, obviously those squares are no longer under the knight's control.

166 □ Can a square be strengthened when a piece moves off it?

A piece doesn't guard itself or the square it occupies. On moving away, it guards the square it just left unless weakened in its new position by being pinned or assuming some other tactical burden.

Though unable to guard itself, a piece can ward off an attack from a piece of like power by capturing the attacker. But if attacked by a piece of a different type, it's helpless to defend itself from that attack.

A rook, for example, can't guard against diagonal attack, nor can a queen, a rook, or a bishop counter an attacking knight. In those cases, the attacked piece can be saved by defending with something else or by delaying defense and first unleashing a more immediate counter-threat. But it's usually simpler to move away, thereby protecting the square once occupied.

167 □ Since the queen can attack in all directions and is the most powerful piece, is it the best defender of an attacked unit?

At first it might seem so, since the queen is the most powerful piece. But actually pawns are better defenders than heavy pieces (queen and rooks), because tying down a pawn to a protective chore is more economical than using a queen or a rook for that purpose.

The minor pieces (bishops and knights) fit neatly between heavy pieces and pawns. They are good attackers and good defenders, which is why in the opening it's imperative to activate them expeditiously.

168 □ Since a queen is the most powerful weapon on the board, why shouldn't I make as many queens as possible?

Usually the presence of one extra queen is sufficient to force an immediate win. In those instances where promoting to a second extra queen is favorable, by all means do so.

But most of the time a second extra queen just gets in the way, especially in games between novices. In fact, you never see good players with more than two queens. They get an extra queen and head straight for mate! A player who makes queen after queen reveals a technique that isn't good enough to win even with material overkill. Mating with an extra queen is one of the first skills a player should learn.

Too much queening also increases the chances of stalemate. With a lethal flotilla on the board, the enemy king may not have any safe moves. If the remaining enemy forces can be ditched with time-gaining moves, a stalemate could pop up unexpectedly.

The object of a chess game is to force a win as soon as possible. Making two or three extra queens wastes time and gives the enemy unnecessary chances. You might even lose if your opponent can exploit the time wasted in creating the queen surfeit to drum up deadly counterchances.

169 □ Since a queen is significantly more valuable than other pieces, why would I underpromote?

Underpromotion is almost always done for tactical purposes. In some instances, promoting to a queen stalemates the opponent. Rather than force a draw, you might prefer underpromoting to a rook, a bishop, or a knight. It's possible, of course, to give stalemate even by promoting a rook. In those cases, you may prefer to make a new minor piece instead. (If time and circumstances allow, you might consider delaying promotion for a move or so, so you can make a queen without giving stalemate.)

Another reason to underpromote is specifically to get a knight in order to win material by giving a forking check. Also, promoting to a knight could gain a key tempo. You don't want to promote to a queen if you get checkmated on the next move. What good is the extra queen in such cases? But by promoting to a knight and giving check, your opponent's plans are at least momentarily thwarted. A final reason to underpromote to a knight is to give immediate checkmate.

Sometimes a bishop can stand in for a queen if a diagonal threat is needed, or a rook if rank-and-file power is required. But nothing really can replace a knight, since its movement is quite different from those of the other units.

170 □ Which piece is the most vulnerable to promotion combinations?

The knight is the weakest link in most promotion combinations, tending to be relatively helpless when attacked by a seventh-rank pawn about to queen. In this case, the pawn is threatening to queen at two places: the square directly ahead of the pawn and the square diagonally ahead, occupied by the knight.

The knight is unable to move out of attack while also positioning itself in time to stop promotion. (It needs two moves to guard an adjacent square on the same rank or file.) The defender's only hope in such instances is to move the knight in a time-gaining way (perhaps by giving check) and then to reposition it a move later to guard the promotion square.

The queen is less vulnerable to promotion combinations than the knight because it has so many potential ways to save itself with time-gaining checks and threats. The king, though often vulnerable to mate by promotion on its home rank, at least has the ability to defend itself from a pawn attack by capturing the pawn (if it's unguarded).

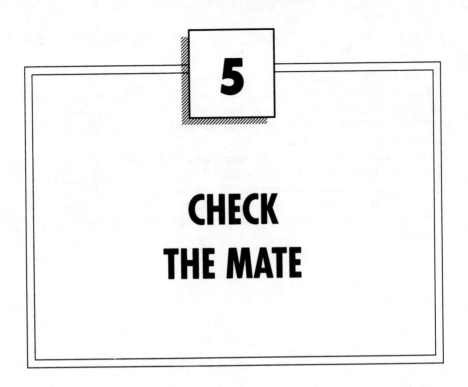

5

CHECK
THE MATE

GETTING THE BASICS

171 □ What is a forcing variation?

A forcing variation is a line of play that forces the other side to make strictly determined moves because any deviation (if any is possible) leads to dire consequences. The forcing side directs the play by giving checks or making strong threats (usually to capture something), which greatly limits the enemy's responses.

172 □ What are the four fundamental ways I can checkmate?

You can checkmate by: (1) attack along a rank or file with a queen or a rook; (2) attack along a diagonal with a queen or a bishop; (3) a supported piece or pawn on a square next to and attacking the enemy king; or (4) attack by a knight.

The first two mates (queen and rook or queen and bishop) can be long-range, since bishops, rooks, and queens attack from a distance. The last two (support and knight mates) are short-range checkmates, with the units acting in close proximity to the enemy king.

173 □ What is a support mate?

The support mate is given by a piece or pawn occupying a square adjacent to the mated king, in which the mating unit is protected by any other friendly unit. The mated king, though close enough to capture the checking unit, can't do so because it may not move into check. Any unit (except the king) can give a support mate under appropriate circumstances, providing it's up close and protected. (Though the attacking king can't itself give mate, it can support the unit that does.)

174 □ What is a back-row mate?

The back-row mate falls into a larger category known as corridor mate, in which either a queen or rook mates by checking along a clear line (rank or file). Corridor mates delivered along an outside row are called back-row mates or back-rank mates, even when the outside mating row is a file.

175 □ What is the difference between a mating attack and a mating net?

Both the mating attack and mating net are directed against the enemy king. The object in both cases is to bring about checkmate.

If a mating net exists, mate is forced against all possible defensive moves, including the very best. Checkmate can be foreseen and demonstrated all the way to the final move.

(The great English champion J. H. Blackburne probably holds the unofficial record for the longest mating net. He announced a forced checkmate in sixteen moves during one of his blindfold exhibitions.)

By contrast, a mating attack is a general offensive against the king that doesn't necessarily result in immediate checkmate. Mate might ensue against inferior defenses, but not necessarily against the most resourceful efforts. In those cases, the attacker may settle for a gain of material, which is sacrificed by the opponent to blunt the ferocity of the mating attack or simply to end it.

IMPOSSIBLE DREAMS

176 □ What is the least amount of material needed to force checkmate against a lone enemy king?

The minimum force needed to insure checkmate is a rook. That is, a king and a rook can mate a lone king by force, no matter how strong the player with the lone king is or how clever the defense, as long as the side with the rook plays the best possible moves (weaker moves usually work here, too). This pattern has been analyzed in its entirety and can be calculated with mathematical certainty.

You can force mate also with king and queen vs. lone king; king and two bishops vs. king; and king, bishop, and knight vs. lone king. These three mates, together with the king and rook mate, are the four basic mates.

Many teachers add two other mates to this list: (1) two rooks against king; and (2) queen and rook vs. king. Though not strictly basic mates and though neither requires the support of the friendly king, they're simple and clear, and display the power of the pieces in their purest form, as do the four traditional basic mates. Everyone should know how to execute them, too.

177 □ Why can't I force mate with a lone bishop or knight?

Because it's impossible; you can't even do it with your opponent's help! See for yourself: on an empty chessboard, place the defending king on a corner square (usually the easiest place to mate the king) and put your own king and minor piece on nearby squares. You can achieve a stalemate but not a checkmate. You can check the enemy king with your minor piece all you like, but the king will always have at least one escape square.

178 □ How can a king and a queen force mate against a lone king?

Generally, the queen is used to force the enemy king to the edge of the board, where the queen keeps it trapped by standing on the next row. The attacking king then moves nearer and eventually occupies a square, on the third row in from the same edge close enough to insure mate. Finally, when the attacking pieces are in position (preferably, though not necessarily, with the two kings opposing each other directly), mate is delivered by the queen along the edge (a back-row mate) or up close to the enemy king on a square protected by the attacking king (a support mate).

179 □ How do a king and a rook beat a lone king?

If it's the attacker's turn to move, a king and a rook can always force mate against a lone king. The process is slightly slower than forcing mate with a king and a queen because the rook, unlike the queen, can be approached and threatened diagonally by the enemy king.

Generally, the rook and king work together to drive the enemy king to the board's edge and confine it there. A support mate is impossible with these forces, since the enemy king always has a free square to the right or left of the check. So the mating check is delivered along an outside row by the rook, with the attacking king necessarily guarding the escape squares not controlled by the rook.

180 □ When a king and a rook mate a lone king, what does the mating position look like?

The mated king always occupies a square on an outside row, and usually the mating king directly opposes it on the same line (the same rank or file), so that one square separates the two kings. Both kings, in this situation, occupy squares of the same color.

Mate is delivered by the rook along the same outside row occupied by the enemy king. To picture this, imagine a right triangle drawn through the three pieces, with the enemy king at the base corner of that triangle.

Whenever a rook gives a right-triangle check, it drives back the enemy king an entire row. If the check occurs on an outside row, that's mate, because there's no row available for retreat. On such a check, the attacking king guards the three squares between itself and the defending king, preventing it from moving forward. The victim is up against the wall with no place to go.

181 □ When a king and a rook mate a king (on an otherwise empty board), do the pieces always line up in a right triangle?

Not always. If the defending king occupies any of the four corners, a rook check along an edge can still be mate even if the two kings are not in line. But the attacking king has to be close enough to guard the possible escape squares not attacked by the rook. Obviously, the corner reduces the defending king's mobility, giving the attacking forces opportunities that don't exist in other configurations.

If defending in such cases, avoid the edges and especially the corners—points of no return.

182 □ How do I win with a king and two bishops against a lone king?

Start by getting your forces centralized and organized. Develop all three pieces to the middle, and especially line up the bishops on adjacent squares, on the same rank or file, so they form a barrier, a wall of protected squares that the enemy king can't cross. The bishops safeguard each other, for the enemy king can't move close enough to attack them. When all three pieces line up, it's called a "big wall."

Then, step by step, drive the enemy king toward the board's edge. A vital weapon in this procedure is a "drive-back" maneuver in which the outside bishop, supported by its king, slants one square up the board toward both kings, forcing the enemy king to step back a row. Repeat this process, forming a new wall and following with a drive-back maneuver, until you trap the enemy king along the edge (make sure to keep the enemy king trapped while avoiding stalemate).

Once the enemy king is imprisoned on an outside row, force it toward one of the corners by a different maneuver, in which your bishops guard successive squares along the edge, thereby denying these squares to the enemy king. Throughout, use your king to prevent the defending king from escaping. After your pieces (king and two bishops) are positioned for the final onslaught, when the harried king's terrain is reduced to two squares, first check with one bishop, forcing the defending king to the corner, then mate by checking with the other bishop. It's a lot harder than it sounds.

FORCING THE ISSUE

183 □ Forcing checkmate with a king, a bishop, and a knight vs. a lone king is actually quite hard, so why is it considered a basic mate?

It's a basic mate because of the pure use of the pieces and because there's a definite technique to force it. The process, however, is a very precise and intricate one, frequently taking thirty moves or more. When executing it, you must be especially watchful to avoid careless moves, for if you exceed the fifty-move rule, your opponent can claim a draw.

184 □ Can a king and two knights force mate against a lone king?

Although it can't be forced, checkmate can be set up with the lone king occupying a corner square (or some other square along the board's edge). In the corner, the winning plan fails because stalemate occurs one move prior to checkmate, the attacker needing an unavailable tempo to reposition the mating knight. Furthermore, the attempt to mate along the edge is also doomed, for it requires the defender to make unnecessary concessions before blundering on the final move, allowing the unforced mate. Most enlightened chessplayers know this ending to be a draw.

185 □ In the previous situation (king and two knights vs. king), does the addition of an extra defending pawn increase winning chances for the knights?

Surprisingly, yes. The presence of a pawn makes things worse for the defender, for it allows the attacker to trap the king without giving stalemate.

The winning attempt requires the pawn to be blockaded by one of the knights, which both obstructs the pawn and contributes to the entrapment of the enemy king. At the right moment, when the enemy king is on its last legs, the blocking knight suddenly enters the attack, permitting the pawn to move without risk of queening. While the pawn is advancing, the knights have time to maneuver into position for the final coup. Sometimes the pawn may even be allowed to queen if mate follows immediately, but these endings are rare and quite difficult. If you ever get one of these in a game, let me know about it.

186 □ What happens when a king and a queen face off against a king and another piece, with no pawns on the board?

Unless there's an immediate tactic allowing checkmate or the capture of the other side's queen, king and queen vs. king and queen is a draw. King and queen vs. king and any other kind of piece (rook, bishop, or knight) is a win, assuming there's no way for the weaker side to exploit the position at hand.

187 □ How do I win when I have a king and a queen, my opponent has only a king and a rook, and there are no pawns on the board?

With such an advantage, you should play to win the opponent's rook. With the rook out of the way, it should take no more than ten moves to force checkmate. The hard part, however, will be winning the rook.

If separated from its king, the rook can usually be picked off by a series of checks leading to a fork. A smart defender gets around this by trying to keep the rook protected by the king. The attacker must try to force them apart to set up a winning double attack, which could take thirty or more moves. The attacking king and queen inch in to drive the enemy king and rook to the edge of the board, to create *zugzwang* (see next question), forcing the rook away from its king, and to conclude with a winning queen fork (an unanswerable simultaneous check to the king and attack on the rook).

188 □ What's *zugzwang*?

Zugzwang is a hapless situation in which any move at all causes a catastrophe to the player's position. The superior side tries to place the opponent in *zugzwang* (without a good move) to capitalize on advantages. The defender tries to avoid *zugzwang* at almost all costs.

Some writers, particularly referring to the endgame, define *zugzwang* to mean neither player wants to move. A move by the inferior side would lose, and one by the superior side would throw away an advantage, resulting in a draw. But in common chess parlance, *zugzwang* refers to one player's desire to avoid having to move when all moves are bad.

189 □ How should I defend when I have a king and a rook against my opponent's king and queen?

Don't panic! There's a chance to draw, even though the ending is a theoretical loss. Keep your head. Your best ally is the fifty-move rule. Place enough obstacles in your opponent's way so that mate or winning your rook in fifty moves becomes difficult. Moreover, a careless or tired opponent may accidentally permit a threefold repetition of position. (In a tournament game, double-check yourself to keep accurate score or you won't be able to claim a draw once the fifty moves are up or when the position is repeated for a third time.)

On defensive technique: keep your king and rook together and in the center, where you can't be mated. If you're gradually driven back, try to erect a barrier with your rook, placing it on the third row in from the edge toward which your king is being driven. This barrier can be breached only by the most exact play. Finally, if everything fails and you're driven to the edge, look for one last sucker punch—a rook sacrifice that forces your poor opponent to stalemate you. It's worth a try.

190 □ King and bishop vs. king and bishop: what's the result?

This situation should end in a draw, regardless of which color squares the bishops use. When the bishops travel on the same color, mate can't even be set up. When the bishops move on opposite colors, mate can be arranged, but only with collaboration.

191 □ Are a king and a pawn sufficient mating material?

A king and a pawn vs. a king are sufficient mating material, not because of the pawn, but because of what the pawn can become upon reaching the last row: a queen or a rook. An actual checkmate with king and pawn vs. lone king can't even be set up.

192 □ If I have a king and a minor piece against a king and a pawn, can't I set up checkmate?

Actually, a mate with king and minor piece vs. king and pawn is possible, but it can't be forced, unless it's a rook-pawn with sure mate already set up in the position. Mate could also result if your opponent underpromoted (why would anyone do this?) and then played some bizarre moves allowing your king and minor piece to give mate in the corner. But you're more likely to find identical snowflakes than a way to win such a game.

193 □ Are there any forced wins requiring more than fifty moves to win, and therefore automatically exceeding the fifty-move limit?

There are various technical positions requiring more than fifty moves to win. If you can demonstrate that there is a win and that it necessitates breaking the fifty-move rule, the tournament director has the discretion to allow you double the number of moves it would take to mate, assuming both sides play the best moves. The same rule generally applies to casual play, although without a tournament director to arbitrate the process, it's hard to get your opponent to agree to jeopardize the chance to draw. Talk fast.

194 □ What is a smothered mate?

A smothered mate is a mate given by a solo knight, in which the victim king is completely blocked by its own forces and has no move, legal or illegal. The mating knight checks "over" the obstacles to do the job.

Regarded by many as the most beautiful checkmate of all, the smothered mate is often given to a victim king trapped in its kingside corner by an enemy knight checking from the loser's king-bishop-two square. When the mate is forced by a series of checks leading to a queen sacrifice on the loser's king-knight-one square, it acquires the special designation "Philidor's Legacy," after the great French player François-André Danican Philidor (1726–95). Philidor had nothing to do with either the mate's creation or original publication, but apparently Thomas Pruen thought so in his 1804 chess book and the name stuck.

PRINCIPAL PRINCIPLES

THE SITUATION AS IT DEVELOPS

195 □ What are the phases of a game of chess?

There are three phases in chess: the opening, the middlegame, and the endgame. These phases are not separated by clear boundary lines but subtle transitions.

The opening, usually the first ten to fifteen moves, is a developing phase: the forces are mobilized, the kings castled, and the center is occupied or controlled.

The middlegame, or second phase, is delineated by planning and its implementation, the goal being to accumulate advantages.

The third and final phase, the endgame, features simplification to exploit tangible and positional superiority. The inferior side meanwhile tries to complicate the issue, keep the position alive, and stave off ignominious defeat.

196 □ What is a principle and its basic purpose?

A principle is a general truth, serving as a guideline for reasonable play. Its purpose is to steer thinking in the right direction. Principles can be very helpful when you don't know what to do. They escort you through unknown territories.

197 □ Starting from any opening, what is White's plan and what is Black's?

White hopes to use the first-move advantage to build a greater superiority and maintain the initiative into the middlegame. Black tries to neutralize White's first-move advantage, hoping to equalize by the middlegame. Theoretically, therefore, White is playing for a win and Black for a draw. In reality, however, a strong player handling Black looks for ways to seize the initiative and steal the advantage.

198 □ What's the most important strategic objective in the opening?

The first thing to do in the opening is to develop the pieces—effectively, harmoniously, expeditiously. In achieving this goal, take special note of your king's safety, and keep your focus on the center of the board. That's where the action is.

199 □ What kinds of things should I be trying to do with each move in the opening phase?

Every move should have a purpose. With each move in the opening you should try to: (1) develop a new piece or clear lines for future development; (2) fight for the center, by occupying, attacking, or influencing it; (3) gain space and increase overall mobility; (4) strengthen your position while avoiding weaknesses; (5) pose at least one threat, if not multiple ones; and (6) meet all enemy threats. If you can more or less follow this program, you should be in good shape (at least you won't get mated in four moves).

200 □ What does a good developing move aim to do?

Development in the opening should accomplish a number of things, such as: (1) attacking and/or defending the center; (2) mobilizing a piece to its most effective square; (3) bringing a piece into play in one move; (4) preparing to castle and connecting the rooks; (5) placing a piece on a safe square where it won't be exposed to attack; and (6) coordinating harmoniously so your pieces don't interfere with one another, causing general disarray.

If a piece is blocked and can't be developed, try to open lines for future emergence.

201 □ How should I develop my pieces?

Generally, you should develop your pieces toward the center as quickly as possible. Begin by moving both center pawns. Try not to move a piece more than once before you've moved some of the other pieces (unless the situation definitely calls for it); otherwise you will be wasting valuable time.

Develop the minor pieces before the queen and rooks, and move at least one knight before any other piece (remember, pawns are not pieces), unless the position demands another approach. While developing, try to attack and threaten the enemy, limiting your opponent's reasonable responses. Don't bring out the queen right away, and prepare to castle fairly early.

Above all, don't be rigid. You can disregard any of these suggestions if the given position so requires. No principle, guideline, or maxim ever overrides the situation at hand.

202 □ What is a developing move?

Development of pieces usually involves their transfer to a more effective square. The minor pieces must be moved off the first rank, though this doesn't necessarily apply to the queen and rooks, which can often be developed by shifting them along the first rank to open files or to files that may soon become open.

For pawns, development involves clearing paths for the pieces to come out. For example, after White moves the e-pawn two squares ahead to start the game, the light-square bishop and the queen can be developed along their respective diagonals.

Besides clearing lines for development, another function of a pawn move in the opening is to safeguard the pieces from attacks by impertinent enemy pawns.

203 □ How should I exploit my opponent's poor development and coordination?

If the enemy forces are in disarray, they will have trouble coping with multiple threats and may be ripe for a combination. Many players expend energy searching for attacks and sacrifices when there is little evidence they exist. But when your opponent's position lacks development and harmony, that's when you should really pore over the board looking for a killer.

If your opponent's pieces are undeveloped, try to open the position, especially by advancing a center pawn. The idea is to create open lines for your own better-developed forces. You should be able to use those lines, but your cramped opponent probably won't. The opponent's best strategy is to keep the position closed to frustrate your attack.

KEEP IT UNDER CONTROL

204 □ In which phase is time most important?

Time is important in all three phases of the game, but if I had to choose one it would be the opening. In the middlegame, if you have a move or two on your opponent, you can gain control of a file, or occupy a key square, or prevent your opponent's plan from being realized, or simply get your attack going first. These are meaningful advantages.

In the endgame, having an extra move can translate to queening first, or getting your king back in time to catch a dangerous pawn, or taking the opposition, or seizing control of a line or square, or being able to make *luft* (creating an escape hatch for the king), among other attractions.

But time advantages in the opening can affect the whole game. If you win right away, there's no middlegame or endgame. Sudden knockouts can happen at any time, but they tend to occur more often in the beginning phase because of developmental disparities—this is why gambits in the opening are so common. The gambiteer might garner several tempi for the pawn and build a winning attack. Give anyone three extra moves and see what happens.

205 □ What does it mean to have the initiative?

The initiative is an advantage in time. The chessplayer forcing the action and directing the flow of play is said to have the initiative.

White has the first move and therefore begins with a natural initiative. Later in the play, the side with the attack has the initiative. The defender must try to squelch the force of the onslaught, seizing the initiative by a sound defense and a well-planned counterattack.

In your own games, whether you play as White or Black, strive to seize or maintain the ability to direct the play. Develop your pieces quickly. Seek opportunities to threaten your opponent in ways that are awkward to counter. And if you have the initiative but don't use it, your opponent will probably take it away from you, and thereby get an advantage.

206 □ What does "playing for the center" mean?

Generally you can play for the center by doing three things, separately or in combination. You can: (1) occupy the center; (2) guard it; and (3) influence it.

You occupy a center square by placing a piece or pawn there. Units cannot defend themselves, however, but must be supported by other friendly forces. You can influence center squares in any number of ways. The primary method is to attack or threaten to attack enemy units aimed at the center. If you then capture, drive away, or nullify those enemy units, you're reducing your opponent's ability to fight in the middle.

207 □ What's the best way to gain control of the center in the opening?

The most effective way to control the center usually is to occupy it with center pawns and to back them up with appropriate piece support. White has a better chance to seize the center initially because of the first-move advantage. Squatter's rights. Try to maintain at least one pawn in the center without having to make significant concessions. If you do, you should hold up your end.

208 □ Why is it better for my pieces to occupy the center?

From the center: (1) pieces attack both wings simultaneously, with greater mobility; and (2) pieces and pawns present a barrier to your opponent, making it difficult to coordinate and develop the opposing forces.

209 □ When my opponent controls the center, how can I fight to equalize it?

The usual way is to counter with a timely pawn advance in the center or just off the center (on a bishop file, for example, trying to swap for an enemy central pawn). In many king-pawn openings, Black can obtain equality by advancing the d-pawn two squares. Under the right conditions, this can neutralize White's e-pawn.

Another idea is to start a flank attack, especially a sudden direct blitz on the enemy king. If anything can stymie your opponent, this is it.

210 □ When it's impossible to challenge my opponent directly in the center or to undertake flank attack, what can I do?

You must somehow attempt to restrain your opponent in the center. Do it this way: (1) trade off your opponent's centralized pieces; (2) prevent the advance of your opponent's center; (3) control the squares immediately in front of your opponent's center pawns.

211 □ Does the principle of centralization apply mainly to the early stages of a chess game?

The principle of centralization is vital throughout a game. True, in the opening you should try to develop to the middle and guard the central squares. But even in the endgame, centralizing the king is paramount. It's more ready to attack and defend key squares while monitoring activities across the board.

Most pieces (though not necessarily rooks) should be centralized in the ending, simply because from the center they radiate in all directions and are more ready to do business anywhere. Queen endings, for instance, can be dominated by a centralized queen, whose power from the center is so great it can thwart its enemy counterpart, denying it access to good squares and a good time.

212 □ How many pawns must I move to develop all my pieces effectively?

Two, your e-pawn and your d-pawn. You can mobilize all your forces productively by moving each center pawn two squares straight ahead. Then, bring the knights toward the center, develop both bishops along clear diagonals, castle, move the queen off the back rank, shift the rooks to the center files, backing up the advance of your center pawns, and achieve the perfect position. Nirvana.

PUT YOUR BEST PAWN FORWARD

213 □ **S**ince most beginners' chess books recommend moving the center pawns two squares each, why do so many strong players use flank openings?

Flank openings can be effective if you understand how to develop them. When you play a flank opening, you might seem to be abandoning the center, but you're really not. You're simply fighting for it in a different way.

The idea is to avoid immediate occupation of the center and to first control it from the flanks and from just off the center. At a later time, when you've gotten a grip on the central squares, you'll want to place your pieces there according to plan.

Flank openings are not recommended for the beginning student because they are harder to grasp. To comprehend them more fully, it's wise to start playing chess by grappling with more traditional approaches to the center. After assimilating those ideas and playing hundreds of games, you can experiment with flank openings and put them to work. Understanding them better, you'll play them better.

214 □ **W**hat are the two main points of attack for White in double-king-pawn openings?

In general, two themes stand out.

The first is the attack against f7: (1) by a bishop from c4 or b3; (2) by a queen from h5 or from d5 or b3, often in battery with a light-square bishop; (3) sometimes by a rook from f1, usually after castling and the exchange of White's f-pawn; (4) and by a knight from g5, sometimes from e5.

The second is the attack against e5: (1) by a knight from f3; (2) by a pawn from d4; (3) sometimes by a pawn from f4; (d) or indirectly, by developing the light-square bishop to b5; attacking the defending knight at c6, pinning it or threatening to capture it.

215 □ What are Black's main goals in double-king-pawn defenses?

Black's main goals interact with White's. Black wants to: (1) safeguard f7 from attack, specifically by developing the g8-knight to f6, which guards h5 and supports the advance d7-d5, closing the a2-g8 diagonal from bishop and queen attack; (2) keep pace with White's development, making sure to mobilize the kingside pieces quickly; (3) prepare to castle early, so Black's king doesn't get trapped in the middle; (4) uphold the king-pawn, retaining a fair share of the center; and (5) prepare the eventual advance of the d-pawn to d5, to neutralize White's e-pawn, establishing central equality.

216 □ Why should I clear the back rank quickly when developing?

Generally, you should clear it rapidly so you can castle if danger threatens. Also, for the rooks to come into play effectively, communicating with and protecting each other, the back rank must be free of obstacles. Then you can safely use your rooks to oppose an enemy rook along an open file, for each supports the other.

The process of clearing the back row for the rooks to cooperate is called "connecting the rooks." When "connection" occurs it usually signals that development is complete, the opening stage is over, and the middlegame is about to commence.

217 □ Why is castling generally desirable?

At almost any point in the beginning stages, the center could open. A king remaining in the region could then be subject to attack, so one reason for castling is to remove the king from potential danger and shelter it behind a wall of pawns.

Additionally, castling activates a rook. After castling, the castled rook can take advantage of the open lines in the middle. If you castle to develop your rook, you're not necessarily castling for defensive reasons. (Indeed, it's sometimes possible to castle and give mate.)

An uncastled king can be a real problem in other ways too, because on its original square it obstructs the pieces. You'll want to castle just to improve your piece harmony. If the front rank is otherwise clear (no minor pieces and no queen in the way), castling connects the rooks, allowing them to defend and support each other for all kinds of operations. In fact, once the rooks are connected, the first stage of opening play is regarded as over, and the real battle begins.

218 □ Is kingside castling better than queenside?

Kingside castling is easier but not necessarily better than queenside castling. Which side to castle on is relative to the position at hand; sometimes it's preferable not to castle at all.

In choosing which side to castle on you should consider: (1) threats to your king's immediate position; (2) how safe your future castled position will be; (3) on which side your opponent's king is castled; (4) whether the center is totally blocked, partially open, or wide open; (5) how soon castling can be completed; and (6) how you expect the attack to proceed.

KING OF THE CASTLE

219 □ Why is kingside castling more common?

Kingside castling is easier and faster. You don't want your king caught in the middle and subject to attack, especially in open games, when attacks can develop suddenly through the center. For this reason, you'll want to prepare to castle fairly early in the game.

To castle kingside, you need to get two pieces off the back rank and out of the way: the king-knight and the king-bishop. Castling queenside requires both the development of two minor pieces and the queen. That additional tempo can be critical. Very often you don't have time to move the queen meaningfully, or you don't want to move it even if you've the time. Castling kingside is less hassle and, unless other factors prevail, usually what you'll think of doing first.

220 □ When I have a choice of castling kingside or queenside, what should I do?

If you have the time, and can wait a move or two, don't hurry to castle either way. Let your opponent commit first. Then you have the option of castling the other way and commencing a pawn storm (a wild advance of several pawns) in front of the enemy king, something you'd ordinarily avoid when your own king is castled on the same side.

After your opponent's castled, if you decide against the pawn storm you may still be able to achieve relative safety by castling on the same side as your opponent, who, like you, probably won't want to be exposed to reckless pawn advances.

221 □ Although the principle is to castle early, are there times when castling should be postponed?

When you can do so without risk, castling may be delayed under these conditions: (1) the tactics allow a gain in attack or initiative; (2) the correct strategy is unclear and you'd rather wait for your opponent to commit to a definite plan before you choose a castling side; and (3) for the moment your king seems safe in the middle, and castling would subject it to a menacing assault.

Generally, keep the king in the middle if it's safe and if: (1) you're headed toward the endgame or already in it (especially when queens have been exchanged); (2) the center is blocked and you're planning to use the flanks for pawn advances and attack; (3) the flanks are more dangerous and the center is obstructed and relatively safer; and (4) the tactical usefulness of keeping the king in the center outweighs everything else in the situation at hand.

222 □ When shouldn't my king be kept in the middle?

Keeping it there is usually not a good idea. But it's especially undesirable if: (1) the center is open, your opponent is castled, and your king can be harassed along the e-file by a major piece (rook or queen); (2) you've lost the right to castle and are subject to attack from various enemy pieces; and (3) your king's presence in the middle disrupts the harmony and development of your forces, particularly the connection of the rooks.

223 □ Why is it usually not a good idea to bring the queen out early in the game?

The queen is high in value, and every time it's attacked by a lesser enemy unit, it must be saved from capture. With each threat to your queen, your opponent can build the position by bringing out a different piece. This means your own development will lag, you'll lose the initiative and may even drop material. You could even get mated.

The queen is a substantial part of your attack force. In the early stages of a game, it's best to keep it in reserve. Develop your queen when you have a better sense of how it will be most effective.

THE QUEEN'S DEBUT

224 □ Is it ever wise to bring the queen out early?

Occasionally you can activate the queen early to punish your opponent's brashness. If the other side has made a series of overly ambitious opening mistakes, for instance, the only way to exploit these errors may be to exercise the queen at once. Otherwise, your opponent may get away with flagrant transgressions. In such a case, your queen could help to force a win. But if the situation is unclear, don't bring the queen out so fast. Stick to good old principles and develop the minor pieces first.

225 □ Where's the best place to position my queen?

The queen exerts the most influence from the center of the board, where it radiates in all directions and can observe as many as twenty-seven different squares. But don't put your queen in the center without careful consideration. You could lose it.

In every phase of the game a centralized queen can be enormously powerful. In the endgame, where your queen faces off against its rival, you'll want to centralize your queen as a dominant principle. In the center, your queen impairs the opposing queen's function, whether in attack or defense, by guarding many of the squares the enemy queen would like to use.

In the earlier phases, it's tricky to keep your queen in the center. You may be able to get it there, but keeping it there could be a problem. Generally, the enemy is able to attack a centralized queen with minor pieces or pawns, forcing a withdrawal. You'll wind up losing time, space, and maybe your queen.

Always be wary of bringing out your queen too early, especially to the center. However, if logic supports it and you can get away with it, move your queen to the center and keep it there, at least until it's gained some kind of advantage.

226 □ Should I avoid an early exchange of queens?

Everything in chess depends on circumstances. You can trade the queen at any point (opening, middlegame, or endgame) when such a transaction is beneficial. There is no particular principle militating against or in favor of trading queens.

Many newcomers avoid exchanging queens because they think of "her" as Superwoman, and tend to overuse her. Winning a chess game, however, may involve using all your forces. Get into the habit of utilizing minor pieces. You'll be surprised and pleased at what they can accomplish alone or in concert with the queen's strength.

227 □ Where are the best places to develop my knights?

Specific opening systems require particular knight placements, but usually it's best to develop them toward the center, placing them on the third square of a bishop file (f3 and c3 for White, f6 and c6 for Black).

So perched, knights attack the most squares possible (eight). Compare this to knight developments to the third squares on the rook files (h3 and a3 for White, h6 and a6 for Black). From such posts, knights attack only four squares. Ergo the maxim "a knight on the rim is dim" and the principle "develop your knights toward the center."

DO IT—DON'T DO IT

228 □ Why would I want to fianchetto a bishop?

You fianchetto a bishop when you develop it on the flank, generally to a knight-two square, where it attempts to attack the center and to control a diagonal running through the middle of the board. You'd make such a development if it were your plan to control the center from a distance without occupying it initially.

The fianchetto is a contemporary approach. A more traditional method, though not an inferior one, is to develop a bishop close to the center or actually in it.

229 □ I've played my bishop to g5, pinning an enemy knight at f6, knowing that if my opponent plays the rook-pawn to h6, I'll retreat the bishop to e3. Don't I waste time by taking two moves to get to a square I could have reached in one?

It may seem so, but a key reason for this type of development is to induce a weakness, a target in the enemy camp. If the enemy moves up the h-pawn, as here, you are provided with a point of attack, and an easier job of opening lines against the castled enemy king. When a pawn moves, it gets closer to the enemy and is therefore more easily exchanged for a hostile pawn. Every pawn exchange creates an open line for potential attack. If the enemy h-pawn has moved, for instance, you can try to open the adjacent g-file by advancing the g-pawn, preferably with rook support, and trading the g-pawn for the h-pawn. Then, double your rooks on the g-file and have a field day.

230 □ Which should I develop first, bishops or knights?

It's not necessary to make even one pawn move to develop both of your knights and begin clearing your back rank. At least two pawns must be moved to develop your two bishops. On the other hand, knights take longer to reach the enemy position and tend to have fewer options in the opening. It's therefore less committal to develop a knight to the third square on a bishop file. Determining the best spot for the accompanying bishop may require waiting a move or two. This explains the maxim "knights before bishops."

But it's not a principle to worship rigidly; all such decisions should be based on the immediate position. Developing both knights before either bishop may be totally wrong for the given situation. In some circumstances, it may even be more desirable to move both bishops before any knights.

Different openings have different criteria, so a slightly better formula, at least for double-king-pawn openings, is to move the kingside knight before the kingside bishop, and the queenside knight before the queenside bishop, often in this order. But if the situation requires different responses, you can throw this principle out the window, too. Don't follow principles mechanically unless you want to lose material or get mated.

231 □ What is the best opening move for White to play?

No one knows for sure. At least several moves are absolutely acceptable if you understand their implications and general requirements.

To expedite development, you can't do better than moving the king-pawn two squares, which most teachers recommend to beginners. This lets out the queen and the king-bishop and speeds up possible kingside castling.

But playing the king-pawn out first isn't necessarily the best move. Advancing the queen-pawn two squares is just as good, though perhaps it leads to more difficult positions. Here development usually proceeds more slowly and castling is delayed. Queen-pawn openings tend to be more positional, whereas king-pawn openings are generally more tactical.

You can also do nicely with White by moving the queen-bishop pawn two squares (the English Opening), or by developing the king-knight to f3 (Reti's Opening). These systems are just as good as starting with the king-pawn or queen-pawn but are harder to grasp. Several other opening moves are good, but are even more difficult to understand. If you're a newcomer, it's better to start with the K-pawn or Q-pawn.

232 □ What should I do if my opponent surprises me in the opening?

Assess your opponent's move objectively. If you can't figure it out, develop quickly and soundly, and castle as soon as you can.

Avoid complications. Your opponent is probably more familiar than you with the position's intricacies and you'll only wind up in time trouble, still puzzled.

Don't lose heart. Perhaps your opponent may be more conversant with the variation, but imperfectly so, merely remembering a sequence of book moves, and not why they're recommended. You might understand the position better, or, because it's unfamiliar, work harder at trying to grasp it, both of which could make a difference.

233 □ How can I avoid quick losses in the opening?

Obvious ways you can lose a game in a few moves are by tactical oversight, failing to see that your king or queen is threatened or overlooking an opening trap. Barring such pitfalls, short games tend to occur when opening principles are violated.

Your chances to lose quickly increase when you: (1) fail to develop rapidly, especially by leaving the minor pieces and center pawns on their original squares; (2) forget to castle or to prepare to castle; (3) bring the queen out too early and unnecessarily; (4) weaken your position with unproductive pawn moves; and (5) become too material-conscious and neglect your position's basic requirements.

GRAB THAT PAWN

234 □ What is pawn-grabbing?

Pawn-grabbing is the pursuit of material gain (namely, enemy pawns) at the expense of time and/or position. In the opening stages, especially, the pawn-grabber inevitably falls behind in development. And if the grabber's king is still uncastled, the problem is compounded.

It's silly to use a queen to snatch a relatively unimportant wing pawn, such as the b-pawn, because this exposes your most valuable asset to danger and also removes it from play without sufficient recompense.

But when the goal is to grab center pawns, the story changes. Acquiring a center pawn may imply important territorial gains, though the piece performing the capture (preferably not the queen) may find itself in the thick of the action. The main danger of usurping center pawns is the possibility of losing several tempi in development or leaving the king uncastled, particularly when the opponent's king has already castled. It's then often wiser to forgo the center pawn's capture and proceed with development, getting the king to safety in the process.

235 □ How much time does pawn-grabbing usually cost?

Pawn-grabbing often wastes three or more tempi. For example, consider a queen trying to rip off a b-pawn (commonly called a poisoned pawn). It's not unusual to waste one turn shifting the queen into position to attack the pawn, a second move capturing the pawn, and a third tempo to bring the queen back to civilization. In the time it takes to set up and take this pawn, the other player could have made three unopposed building or menacing moves. These three moves can give your opponent a winning advantage.

236 □ What are some typical ways to waste time (moves) in chess?

You can waste time by: (1) exchanging an already developed piece for an undeveloped one; (2) allowing one of your units to be attacked by a less valuable enemy unit; (3) winning material, especially by pawn-grabbing.

237 □ What should I aim to do in the early part of a game?

Casual players often want to know how to play the opening better, what to strive for, and what to avoid. The biggest gains in playing strength can be achieved by learning how to get a solid game in the initial ten moves.

The first thing is to develop your pieces. In the opening, nothing is more important than mobilizing your forces, especially by moving your two center pawns (advancing at least one of them two squares) and bringing out your knights and bishops, which should be positioned in and around the center.

Make sure to castle. If the center is opened, your king is likely to become exposed. Enemy pieces will find it easier to attack your king when it stays on its home square. When castling, you should attempt to place your king behind a wall of shielding pawns while enabling your rooks to come to the central files.

Make only useful or necessary pawn moves. Advancing the e- and d-pawns fights for the center and also releases the pieces on the home rank. Most other pawn moves generally contribute less to building your game and may actually weaken your position. They tend to waste time, which could be used to bring out knights and bishops. After castling, be careful about pushing the pawns in front of your king, which could encourage enemy invasion.

Try to save the queen for later. Early queen play often leads to a loss of time. Since the queen is the most valuable unit, it has to be moved to safety practically every time it's attacked. Bringing out the queen early to grab a meaningless pawn (pawn-grabbing) isn't solid opening play, because in the three or four moves needed to grab the pawn your opponent might be able to mobilize an armada of weapons to sink your king. You win a pawn, but get mated: crime and punishment.

DON'T DO IT—DO IT

238 □ What are some of the important don'ts in the opening?

One could almost write a book on pitfalls alone! Don't: (1) make unnecessary pawn moves; (2) bring out the queen too early; (3) move a piece twice in the opening; (4) trade a developed piece for an undeveloped one; (5) exchange without good reason; (6) develop just to bring a piece out and not with a specific purpose; (7) block your center pawns; (8) impede the development of your pieces; (9) weaken your king's position or move your uncastled king; (10) move knights to the edge of the board; (11) waste time (or moves); (12) indulge in pawn-grabbing; (13) sacrifice without good reason; (14) refuse a sacrifice because your opponent made it quickly and confidently (analyze it, then decide); (15) play without a plan or develop in an uncoordinated way; (16) change plans from move to move; (17) remain uncastled too long; (18) advance pawns too far too soon; (19) ignore your opponent's moves; (20) give pointless checks; (21) capriciously avoid making natural captures or recaptures; (22) take your opponent too lightly or too seriously; (23) play a set order of moves without regard to your opponent's responses; and (24) open the center with your king still uncastled.

On the other hand, don't follow any of the above too religiously, for chess is a dynamic game that requires real thinking in each position. Knowing the precepts alone doesn't win a chess game. You also must play strong moves.

239 □ What's the shortest possible game of chess?

Two moves: two for White and two for Black. It's called the Fool's Mate, and it's White who gets mated along the e1-h4 diagonal by the black queen. White is unable to block out the queen because of premature f-pawn and g-pawn advances. To inflict the same kind of mate on Black, it would take White three moves. In either case, the mate is achieved not because of the stellar play of the winner but because of the horrendous errors by the loser.

240 □ Are the Scholar's Mate and the Fool's Mate the same thing?

Both refer to short chess games, but they are actually quite different. In a Scholar's Mate, White's queen, supported by a bishop at c4, captures on f7, giving mate in no less than four moves after the game starts. Both White and Black play badly: Black by failing to see White's threats, resulting in a four-move loss; White by prematurely developing the queen.

A Fool's Mate results after two blunderous pawn moves. By advancing the pawns to g4 and f3. White allows Black's queen an easy mate from h4, because White has no way to block the check. In this case, only White plays badly. Black is merely lucky.

In neither the Scholar's Mate nor the Fool's Mate does the winner play well. In the Fool's Mate, Black has good fortune; in the Scholar's Mate, White gets away with murder. Both mates can be played with reversed colors, but regardless of who mates whom, it seems fools, more than scholars, get the last laugh.

241 □ Doesn't the stronger player need fewer moves to win a chess game?

We assume a strong player attempts to force a win as quickly as possible, but this isn't necessarily the fastest way to win. Sometimes weaker players win more quickly by taking chances that risk defeat. If the opponent fails to refute their unsound play, the game ends quickly, maybe in ten moves or less.

When I hear that someone wins a lot of games in under ten moves, I figure it's mainly luck. Stronger players may take twenty or thirty moves to win in the same situations because they're being careful. But they'll win a greater percentage of the time, and they'll throw away fewer winning positions.

242 □ Is it possible to play the opening with the goal of achieving a favorable endgame?

The opening and endgame can't be separated. The endgame is actually the logical outcome of everything that came earlier, beginning with the opening. Formations created in the first few moves of a contest can last right down to the end of a game, many moves later. This is especially true with regard to pawn structure. Pawns can only move forward. Once made, you're stuck with a pawn move and its consequences.

If you're willing to play for the endgame from the start, try to simplify. Especially try to trade queens to some advantage, however minimal, and to exchange bad minor pieces for good ones. Also keep in mind the need to set up favorable pawn imbalances, in which a group of your pawns confronts a smaller number of enemy pawns. This you do by making exchanges that induce weaknesses or creating useful pawn majorities.

243 □ Which is the most difficult phase to study?

There's room for argument, but it's likely the middlegame is the hardest.

The opening is easier to learn because you get plenty of practice with it. Every game has an opening, but not always a middlegame or endgame. Openings always start with the same position, and it's easier to commit such matters to rote memory, whether you understand them or not.

The endgame, with fewer units on the board, is also an easy phase in which to classify information. For example, if you have a bishop-vs.-knight ending, you can look up the appropriate section in almost any endgame book and find out which conditions favor the bishop and which the knight. You can also memorize certain key positions or themes that commonly occur. Other identifying characteristics may also stand out.

The middlegame doesn't fit as nicely into simple categories to facilitate study. Unlike openings, the starting point is almost never the same, and unlike endgames, the resulting positions are harder to classify and research in a book, because there are numerous units on the board in more complicated situations.

244 □ In which phase is the advantage of an extra pawn most important?

Material advantages tend to be more significant in the endgame. For example, you could gain a piece in the opening but still be outnumbered on the battlefield if none of your forces are active. Upon reaching the endgame, however, laggard development may have been corrected and the superiority of an extra piece really shows. Pawns, in particular, play a greater role in the endgame because they may suddenly have a chance to queen. In the opening, however, pawn promotion is rare.

245 □ If I as a newcomer were to study any particular group of openings, what should it be?

Begin with double-king-pawn openings in which both players start by moving their e-pawns two squares ahead. This will give you the soundest underpinnings.

Double-king-pawn openings stress development, central attack and occupation, mobility, king safety, time, and the initiative. They lead to open games, with clear lines and unblocked centers, abounding in tactics and direct attacks. What you learn from these openings are the hinges on which most games swing, regardless of a competitor's abilities.

After immersing yourself in double-king-pawn theory, you can move on to asymmetrical king-pawn responses, queen-pawn games, Indian systems and flank openings, or whatever strikes your fancy.

246 □ What is the most popular opening in contemporary chess?

Probably no opening is more recognized than the popular Sicilian Defense. It arises after White starts the game by moving the e-pawn from e2 to e4, and Black responds by moving the c-pawn from c7 to c5. First essayed in recorded play by the Italian Polerio in 1594, it stimulates sharp, asymmetrical fights, where Black generally attacks on the queenside and White on the kingside.

White usually wins the shorter games because of an early edge in development. Black's chances improve in the middlegame and endgame, especially if White has overextended the front lines, advancing the pawns too far, leaving behind indefensible weaknesses. But to get this far, Black must survive White's early initiative.

A key to the opening's vicissitudes is that Black often obtains a central pawn majority by exchanging the c-pawn for the enemy d-pawn, with the result that Black has more pawns on the central files than White (a d- and e-pawn vs. an e-pawn). The difficulty is to ward off White's beginning assault until the central majority can be used meaningfully.

247 □ What is a good program of opening study for a casual player?

There are any number of programs, rigid and flexible, that work for the less competitive player. I suggest the following to some of my own students: (1) a general introduction to the principles of open games (history and theory behind double-king-pawn openings, including at least one hundred overview games and three hundred supporting tactical positions, stressing development, center play, the seizing of open lines, and the importance of early castling); (2) some specific opening variations to be committed to memory (taken from a textbook or general opening manual, including variations against every major asymmetrical king-pawn response, and an entire repertoire for Black); (3) some short games from those openings and variations (if they can be found, as many as fifty games for each variation, of no more than thirty moves per game); (4) characteristic middlegame positions resulting from these variations, with an emphasis on typical tactics (including diagrams of twenty to fifty desirable formations per opening studied, and an equal number of diagrams showing positions to avoid); (5) appropriate plans and strategies of these middlegames (listed under each diagram, indicating the functions of each piece, where they should be stationed, and so on); (6) a steady diet of speed chess and practice games, attempting to implement these ideas (where they are tried, against the strongest opposition possible, without regard to results); (7) fully annotated master games in the same openings (fifty to one hundred tournament and match games from contemporary play, analyzed mainly by world-class grandmasters); (8) tournament play, in which these ideas are courageously tried (students must play at least fifty serious tournament games a year, as well as at least fifty serious experimental games to generate information); and (9) an analysis of these games (first by the student, then by a master player or better), to see what was done right and what wrong, and to decide where to go from there—maybe a new set of openings.

248 □ Do any of the older openings, popular in former times, still have value?

A lot of the old lines are just as good if not better now than they used to be. It's natural to think that, since they're out of date, they're not any good or have been superseded. In reality, many of these variations simply fell out of style and were never really refuted.

The classics never grow old. Even a little familiarity with them can constitute a tremendous practical advantage, because few players study them. Many players try only to keep up with the latest wrinkles, which when facing a strong player is like walking into the lion's den.

7

PLOTS, PLANS, AND MACHINATIONS

OPENING LINES

249 □ **H**ow do I know if I have a spatial advantage?

You have a spatial edge in open positions (where movement through the center is possible because at least a pair of central pawns have been exchanged) if: (1) your pieces occupy more centralized posts than your opponent's; (2) your forces attack a greater portion of the board; and (3) you control key files and diagonals leading to the opponent's camp.

You can actually make a mechanical calculation. Count the squares across the frontier line (an imaginary horizontal line dividing the board in half) that your pieces occupy and attack, and compare the number to those the enemy's forces occupy and attack on your side of the midline. A small difference indicates virtual parity, but a large one implies significant spatial dominance.

In closed positions, where movement through the center is impeded by both players' pawns, you tend to have a spatial superiority if your pawns, especially the middle ones, are farther advanced. You would then have more room behind the lines to maneuver, and consequently, your opponent (with less room for maneuvering) would probably be a little cramped.

250 □ If my opponent has a cramped game, how should I proceed?

If your opponent's game is cramped, usually it's best to just keep it that way. Discourage freeing pawn advances and avoid the exchange of pieces. Eventually, enemy units, stepping on their own toes, might fail in one or several defensive tasks. At that point, especially if you've been setting up multiple attacks and threats, your opponent may lose material or simply be unable to guard everything.

While keeping your opponent cramped, look for ways to increase your spatial advantage. Also keep a sharp eye out for pawn advances to drive back enemy pieces (without entailing risk). Generally, the more you advance your pawns, the more room you'll have behind the lines to frolic and gambol.

251 □ What's the remedy for a cramped position?

If you find yourself cramped, try to alleviate the constriction with freeing pawn moves and exchanges of pieces, especially those pieces causing the most problems. But heed a word of caution. Don't open the position if it seems your opponent is better prepared to exploit the clearance than you are. You could be opening a Pandora's box.

On the other hand, if it's your opponent who's cramped, avoid exchanges that would relieve his game. Keep it boxed up, so enemy pieces must step over each other. Use your spatial edge to maneuver your pieces for multiple threats, especially on both flanks. Try to render your opponent optionless and overburdened.

252 □ What are open, half-open and closed files?

An open file has no pawns on it at all, neither enemy nor friendly. It's used to attack the opposition by either side's major pieces (rooks and queen). If there's an open file, you should try to control it.

A half-open (or semi-open) file has a pawn (or pawns) of only one color on it. It can be used for attack only by the side that has none of its own pawns in the way.

A closed file is occupied by pawns of both sides and therefore can't be used by either side's major pieces.

253 □ Is the classification of a file also based on whether it's blocked by pieces?

Pieces don't determine file classification because pieces aren't stationary, as pawns are. Even when a piece or two temporarily blocks a file, the line might suddenly open if the pieces move away or are driven off.

Pawns tend to be the real obstacles, which is why most long-term chess thinking (planning/strategy) is based on their structure.

254 □ What's the value of an open file?

An open file can be used to attack the enemy position or to bring a rook into the game. A rook occupying an open file attacks every square on the file, and may be able to move with advantage to several of them.

For example, on an open file, a rook may suddenly be able to leap to the last rank and give checkmate. Or it could relocate to the seventh rank, wreaking havoc. Alternatively, a rook on an open file could move up to the third or fourth rank for transfer to another sector of the board (a maneuver known as a "rook lift").

Even when immediate movement along an open file isn't possible, the mere presence of the rook guarding every square on it might prevent or deter enemy pieces from moving to the file. Thus, most of the time, simply placing a rook on an open file confers an advantage, which explains the maxim: "Rooks belong on open files."

255 □ How do I go about opening a file for my own use?

You can use a file if none of your own pawns block it or if your rooks and queen can shift in front of an otherwise impeding friendly pawn (such as by a rook lift). When a friendly pawn is in the way, there are essentially two ways to clear the path: (1) a pawn advance and subsequent exchange and/or (2) a sacrifice.

256 □ How do I use a pawn advance to open a file?

Using the pawn-advance method, most of the time you will focus on an enemy pawn that has already moved. You may have to block that pawn with a unit of your own, thereby preventing it from moving out of attack.

After the enemy pawn is blocked (or tactically restrained) and unable to move, attack it with a friendly pawn from an adjacent file. This pawn should be protected by a friendly piece, so when the enemy pawn takes your pawn, you can retake it with that piece—then the file is open for your rooks and queen. If the enemy pawn doesn't take your pawn, then, when desirable, take the enemy pawn with your pawn, which likewise clears the file for your attack.

If this approach doesn't work, and you still want to open the file, you might have to resort to a sacrifice. But be very careful. Make sure to calculate the resulting position to your satisfaction.

257 □ What should I do if my opponent already occupies an open file with a rook?

Perhaps you can place a protected rook of your own on the same file. This reduces your opponent's ability to move along the file, for you would then have the opportunity to capture it with your own rook.

It may be stronger to move your rook to the same file if both of your rooks are still on the board and working together. In that case, one rook, if captured, can be replaced by the other. Sometimes your queen, having the same file-power as a rook, can function in this way, supporting your opposing rook. Other times different pieces, even the king, can support your rook moving to a file already occupied by an enemy rook, especially if your opponent can't exploit the possible exchange of rooks that might then take place.

If you can't oppose the enemy rook with a rook of your own, maybe you can keep the enemy rook from penetrating your position with careful defense. Or even better, seize another open file. Then the threat to achieve counterplay should be enough to keep the game balanced.

258 □ What is a battery?

A battery is a double force, with two friendly pieces of like power attacking in unison along the same line (rank, file, or diagonal). Rank or file batteries consist of two rooks, two queens (rarely), or rook and queen (or queen and rook, since either piece can be first in line). Diagonal batteries sport bishop and queen (or queen and bishop), or two queens (also rare).

A battery is two-ended, in that threats can emanate in either direction along the line of attack, and either piece may capture with its partner's support. Either way, it's assault and battery.

259 □ If there are two or more open files and my opponent already controls one, should I automatically oppose the enemy rook?

Not necessarily. A wiser course might be to seize control of another file, so that rather than attempt to reduce enemy threats you create stronger ones of your own. Your industrious rook can be the key to obtaining a bright future.

260 □ After occupying an open file with a rook, what is my next goal for it?

The seventh rank is a terrific place for a rook. By occupying that rank with a rook you can confine the enemy king to the board's edge and simultaneously blitz a row of several pawns (all the unmoved pawns remain on this rank). Many games are decided by such an incursion.

261 □ What is meant by the seventh rank?

The seventh rank is the next-to-last rank on the board from either player's perspective. When a white rook moves to its seventh rank, we're referring to the rank on which the black pawns begin the game. When a black rook moves to its seventh, we mean the rank on which the *white* pawns start. The meaning depends on the relevant perspective.

262 □ My rook occupies the seventh rank. How can I intensify the pressure?

Double your rooks on the seventh rank! If one is good, two must be twice as good, and if you can't double with a rook, try a queen. A major-piece battery on the seventh is almost always a winning advantage, since it then becomes easier to gain material by support capture, and, if the opposition king is confined to its home rank, to deliver checkmate.

263 □ My opponent has an active, well-posted piece. How should I proceed?

Try to exchange it or drive it to an inferior position. If it's a minor piece (bishop or knight), force its trade for a less effective one. If it's a strong rook on an open file, neutralize it by occupying that same file with your own rook. This challenges the enemy rook, deters it from moving along the file, and certainly reduces its power.

But be careful about initiating a rook trade on an open file if a new enemy rook takes over the post of the old. If you do implement such an exchange, be sure you can safely bring a second rook of your own to the contested file to reestablish the balance.

If, however, you can't negotiate a favorable trade, try to reduce the scope and clout of the enemy piece by forcing a retreat or an undesirable repositioning. Stick a pawn in its face and drive it back.

264 □ Can a knight ever be well placed on the edge of the board?

A knight performs optimally from the center (the box of squares running from c3 to c6 to f6 to f3). Placing it outside this zone usually impairs the knight's function and isolates it.

Still, there are times when it's perfectly proper to move a knight to the edge: (1) to gain a tactical advantage; (2) to disrupt the harmony of the enemy forces; (3) to occupy a protected flank square when the center is blocked; and (4) to use the flank merely as a transfer to a more useful square, especially in the central zone (a typical instance is shifting a white knight from c3 to a4 to c5, where a4 is the transfer square).

265 □ What is a bad bishop?

A bad bishop is blocked by its own pawns and unable to move freely from wing to wing. Bad bishops arise more often in closed positions, where the center is naturally blocked by interlocking pawns. Wherever pawns obstruct diagonals, the scope and value of bishops is likely to be diminished. Knights, on the other hand, may thrive in such circumstances because they can scale barriers and gain a foothold close to the center.

266 □ How can I capitalize on my opponent's bad bishop?

Don't let your opponent trade the bad bishop. Avoid a direct swap if you have a good bishop traveling on the same color squares as the enemy's bad one. If you must trade your good bishop, at least try to exchange it for a valued enemy knight. Without a same-color attacking bishop on the board, the defender may find it even more difficult to get rid of the bad-bishop nuisance.

Moreover, to exacerbate further the bad bishop's condition, trade all the remaining pieces for their equal number on the other side, including the queens and rooks. In general, eliminate all your opponent's effective pieces to highlight the problems of your adversary's inferior one, the bad bishop, leaving nothing on the board to compensate for it.

PAWN-DER THIS

267 □ What is a passed pawn?

A passed pawn is free to move up the board toward promotion without opposition by an enemy pawn. No enemy pawn can block it or guard a square in its path. A passed pawn is generally advantageous because it can produce a new queen. A pawn becomes passed when it actually passes the enemy pawns that might stop its advance, or when those enemy pawns are exchanged off or lured away.

Passed pawns can be: (1) ordinary; (2) outside; (3) protected; (4) connected; or (5) split.

268 □ What is an outside passed pawn?

This pawn, situated away from the main theater, is free to move toward promotion. Threatening to become a new queen, it's typically used to decoy the enemy king to one side of the board, allowing the friendly king to invade on the other wing. The term often applies to endgames when each side has a passed pawn. The pawn "outside," or furthest away, confers advantage.

269 □ What is a protected passed pawn?

Also known as a supported passed pawn, this is a passed pawn guarded by another pawn. A piece (knight, bishop, rook, or queen) can't capture the protected passed pawn without surrendering material, for it could be recaptured by the protecting pawn. Then, even if the second pawn were also captured, the two pawns together (2 points) would not equal a knight (3 points), the least valuable of the pieces. Needless to say, neither do they equal a bishop (3), rook (5), or queen (9).

The chief advantage of a protected passed pawn is that it frees friendly pieces from defensive chores and encourages them to pursue attack. In king-and-pawn endings, particularly, a protected passed pawn restricts the defending king to a localized area. If the king wanders too far, it might not be able to return in time to catch the pawn before it queens.

270 □ What are connected passed pawns?

Connected passed pawns, also called united passed pawns, are two pawns on adjacent files that are both passed, so no enemy pawn can block them or guard squares in their path. Such pawns are free to advance toward promotion, assuming no enemy pieces can hinder them. They are particularly resilient if attacked, for they defend each other: whichever pawn advances is guarded by the pawn remaining a square behind.

Connected passed pawns can be extremely strong. When two of them occupy their sixth rank and confront a lone enemy rook, unless there are immediate saving tactics (or the defending king is close enough to lend a hand), the pawns are unstoppable. Attacked along the rank, either pawn can advance, threatening to make a new queen and effectively preventing the capture of the other.

271 □ What are split passed pawns?

Split passed pawns are two passed pawns of the same color, separated from each other by at least one file. Neither split pawn can be defended by a pawn and therefore both might be vulnerable to piece attack. In guarding them, friendly pieces may be forced to assume passive, defensive roles, losing scope and flagging into general inactivity.

272 □ Are split pawns always a liability?

Sometimes split pawns are more a weapon than a weakness, especially in pure pawn endings (no queens, rooks, bishops, or knights on the board). If both pawns are passed, and also within the enemy king's sector, they can defend themselves by timely advances.

Line the pawns up on the same rank before either is actually attacked by the enemy king. As the king moves in front of one split pawn, threatening capture, push the other up to the same rank as the king. If the king captures the back pawn, it's then out of position to overtake the front one, which advances to become a queen.

273 □ If the enemy king doesn't capture my back split pawn in the previous situation, how do I proceed?

It depends whether your king is close enough and free to protect them, which it should do if it can. If not, and if the enemy king doesn't capture the back pawn but instead retreats to catch the front one (it takes three moves of repositioning to attack the front pawn from that situation), prepare to advance the back one as soon as safety permits. If the enemy king retreats out of range, line up both pawns on the same rank. As before, if either is then attacked, push the other, so that the back one becomes immune from capture.

During this maneuver, it's often necessary for the friendly king to shift tempo by making some nondamaging interim move, preferably toward the split pawns. If the friendly king is tied to defense and unable to temporize, however, the split pawns may lack the power to sail along. They can assume the vulnerable aspects of isolated pawns, made-to-order victims.

274 □ Are split pawns separated by more than a file also able to defend themselves by timely advances?

Split pawns separated by two files often can protect themselves. In fact, if both pawns line up on their own fifth rank, and if neither is under immediate attack, the two pawns working as a team can force a new queen, even without resorting to a time-gaining move by their own king. If split pawns (separated by two files) occupy only their third rank, however, and if the friendly king can't offer help, the enemy king can capture both.

275 □ What is a pawn majority?

As the name implies, a pawn majority is a numerically superior group of pawns. You have a pawn majority if, over any consecutive group of files, you have more pawns than your opponent does.

For instance, if you have two pawns on the e-file and the d-file, and your opponent has a single pawn on the e-file, you have a central pawn majority, two to one. Or if your opponent has three pawns on the f-, g-, and h-files, and you have just two pawns on the same files respectively, your opponent has a kingside majority. (For the purpose of this example, neither side has a pawn on the e-file.)

276 □ When is a pawn majority considered healthy?

A pawn majority is healthy if it consists of no doubled or backward pawns and can therefore produce a passed pawn. If one of your majority pawns is doubled, the value of your pawn majority is lessened because a single enemy pawn may be able to hold back your doubleton, which then functions as if it were one pawn. If your opponent has a healthy majority elsewhere on the board, even though the position might be materially even, you could be, in effect, a pawn down.

277 □ What advantage ensues from a healthy pawn majority?

Once a healthy pawn majority produces a passed pawn, the pawn should be advanced (or prepared for advance) with the eventual threat of promoting. This is possible because no enemy pawn can block the passed pawn's advance or guard a square over which it must pass.

Since no enemy pawn can stop your passed pawn, the enemy pieces will have to do the job, which forces them to assume defensive roles. This should increase the power and possibilities of your own pieces.

If only kings and pawns remain, a passed pawn can signify an even greater advantage. For if the enemy king is lured by the passed pawn's march, enemy pawn groups and other important individual pawns could become totally indefensible to your marauding king.

278 □ How do I best mobilize a pawn majority?

Start the mobilization by advancing the unopposed pawn first, a technique classified as Capablanca's Rule, after José Raoul Capablanca, the third champion of the world (1921–27). He emphasized this principle in several of his books. The unopposed pawn, also known as the candidate passed pawn, has no enemy pawn occupying its file.

If you have pawns on a2, b2, and c2, for example, and your opponent has pawns on a7 and b7, start by advancing the c-pawn to c4. It's a mistake to push the b-pawn first, from b2 to b4. Black could answer with a move of the b-pawn from b7 to b5. That b-pawn then holds back all three White pawns: the one at b4 by blockage, and the ones at a2 and c2 by guarding the squares they would eventually move to, a4 and c4.

One bit of advice. If feasible, your own king should join the mobilizing pawns. It may be needed to support the advancing pawns up the board. Move the pawns without king support, and they may be victimized by the enemy king's looming counterattack.

279 □ How does a pawn majority arise?

Pawn majorities are created either by exchanging or by sacrifice. Kingside/queenside majorities often result when one player captures away from the center, which may give the opponent a majority on the other side of the board. This explains why, in many cases, you should take back toward the center even though doing so isolates a rook-pawn. Capturing toward the center may prevent your opponent from obtaining a workable pawn majority and a treacherous passed pawn.

280 □ What is a queenside pawn majority?

You have a queenside pawn majority if you have more pawns on the queenside than your opponent does—that is, if you have numerical superiority in pawns between the a- through d-files. To have a kingside pawn majority, you would need more pawns than your opponent between the e- and h-files. To exploit either majority, use both sides of the brain.

281 □ What is the advantage of a queenside pawn majority?

A queenside pawn majority, when healthy, can produce a passed pawn. If both players have castled kingside, as usually happens, the player with a queenside majority can use it to produce a passed pawn that lures away the enemy king. Once the defending king leaves the kingside to catch the passed pawn on the queenside, it abandons the kingside pawns to the enemy king.

282 □ For a queenside majority, is it better to have a superiority of two vs. one, three vs. two, or four vs. three?

Generally, the smaller the majority the better, because it then takes less time to mobilize and produce a passed pawn from this group. Moreover, if the majority is a large one (four vs. three or five vs. four), the defending king can more easily add to the resistance when the candidate passed pawn is on a central file (because the king doesn't have to travel as far). Thus two vs. one is preferable to the other two choices, though even better is one vs. nothing, especially when it's an outside passed pawn. (For the purpose of this example, we've excluded majorities of greater disparity, such as three vs. one, and four vs. two, which pose different circumstances.)

283 □ When is a queenside pawn majority less advantageous?

When it's not healthy and when both players have castled queenside. In that case it's better to have a kingside majority, even though, in castling queenside, both players position their kings closer to the center (on the queen-bishop file) than they would if they castled kingside (on the king-knight file). Being closer to the center makes it easier to defend against pawn majorities on the other flank. (For this example, the center consists of the files the queens and kings occupy at the start.)

PAWN CHAINS AND WEAK LINKS

284 □ What is a pawn chain?

In a general sense, a pawn chain is any group of friendly pawns that occupy adjacent files and are connected along the same diagonal.

More specifically, however, it's an interlocking sequence of white and black pawns, with each side's pawns arranged on separate diagonals. None of the pawns can move, each being obstructed by its enemy counterpart.

285 □ What does it mean to develop the bishop "outside the pawn chain"?

It refers to an order of development, whether to move a bishop or a potentially obstructive center pawn first. You prevent your bishop from developing aggressively (lock it "inside the pawn chain") when you advance a center pawn one square, obstructing the bishop's diagonal. You avoid this blockage by moving the bishop first, say to a bishop-four or a knight-five square, and then advancing the center pawn one square. You thus develop your bishop "outside the pawn chain."

286 □ What is the base of a pawn chain?

The base pawn is the least advanced pawn in any diagonally connected sequence of like-color pawns. It is therefore the support of the entire chain.

More specifically, the base pawns (one for White and one for Black) are the least advanced pawns in an interlocking chain of white and black pawns.

287 □ What is the proper way to attack a pawn chain?

According to the theory developed by Aron Nimzovich (1886–1935), a pawn chain should be attacked at its most vulnerable point. The weakest link is the base, the only pawn in the chain not supported by another pawn. If the base falls, the whole thing could topple—like knocking out the first floor of a skyscraper.

288 □ When are pawn chains most likely to result, and how should I proceed when there is one?

Pawn chains typically arise in closed positions, when the center becomes blocked by fixtures of white and black pawns. Since little or no activity can take place in the center itself, try to: (1) play on the flanks; (2) seize all available open lines; and (3) undermine the opponent's center pawns by attacking at the base of the enemy chain.

289 □ Which openings are most likely to generate pawn chains and closed centers?

Pawn chains and closed centers can result from numerous openings, including specific variations in the French Defense, the Closed Ruy

Lopez, the King's Indian Defense, the Nimzo–Indian Defense, the Nimzovich Defense, and certain Benoni lines.

290 □ What is a weakness?

There are two types of weaknesses—tactical and strategic. When a unit or square is insufficiently protected or poorly placed, it's a tactical weakness and could be immediately exploitable. This weakness can often be corrected if there's time.

Strategic weaknesses are defined by pawn structure, meaning a square is weak when, for any reason, it can't be guarded by a pawn. The enemy can try for advantage by occupying or exploiting the weak squares.

291 □ What is the relationship between a hole and an outpost?

A hole is a weak square on a player's second, third, or fourth rank that no friendly pawn can guard but that can be protected by an enemy pawn. An outpost is a strong square on·a player's fifth, sixth, or seventh rank guarded by a friendly pawn and incapable of being guarded by an enemy pawn. It's particularly attractive to friendly pieces because of the anchoring pawn, especially if it's on an open file occupied by a rook. Your outpost is your opponent's hole, and vice versa.

SOME PAWNS ARE ISLANDS

292 □ What are the main pawn weaknesses?

Typical pawn weaknesses include: (1) the isolated pawn (also called an isolani); (2) doubled pawns; (3) doubled isolated pawns; (4) the backward pawn; (5) hanging pawns; and (6) the isolated pawn pair.

The worst place to have pawn weaknesses is in front of the king, for those strategic weaknesses are often tactical ones as well, subject to all kinds of sudden shots and pronged attacks.

293 □ Why should I accept any pawn weakness?

You should be willing to accept a pawn weakness to: (1) get sufficient activity or counterplay for your pieces: (2) gain or maintain an edge in development, time, and/or initiative; (3) build or sustain an attack, or keep up the pressure; (4) increase mobility or space; (5) secure a square, unit, sector, your king, or overall position; (6) implement an immediate tactic; and/or (7) hold an otherwise losing or unfavorable situation. That's chess—accepting minuses to gain pluses.

294 □ What is an isolated pawn?

An isolated pawn is one that can't be protected by a friendly pawn because there is no friendly pawn on an adjacent file. (If there are pawns on adjacent files but they're blocked and incapable of moving to protect an advanced pawn, the advanced pawn then is artificially isolated.) When an isolated pawn is attacked by the enemy, it has to be protected by a piece, often forcing that piece into a defensive role, giving it less participation and reduced importance.

295 □ When is an isolated pawn weak?

An isolated pawn may be weak if the enemy: (1) controls the square immediately in front of it, preventing the pawn's advance; (2) can occupy the square immediately in front of it for use as an attack launching pad; and (3) can pile up on the target with major or minor pieces, forcing friendly pieces to take on defensive chores.

296 □ How should I proceed if I have an isolated pawn?

When saddled with an isolated pawn, try to: (1) build an attack by exploiting the open or semi-open files on either side of the pawn; (2) prevent the pawn from being blockaded; (3) advance it in a timely way, exchanging it for a healthy enemy pawn or to seize more space; (4) avoid trading pieces, resulting in a lifeless endgame; and (5) exploit outpost squares supported by the isolated pawn.

297 □ How should I play against an isolated pawn?

To accentuate its weakness, try to: (1) stop or dissuade its advance; (2) control and occupy the square in front of it; (3) pile up on it with your pieces, especially if its movement is restrained; and (4) exchange off the pawn's best defenders, emphasizing its vulnerability and minimizing counterplay.

298 □ How is the isolated d-pawn different from other isolated pawns?

The isolated d-pawn is unusual because it can be both weak and strong. Typical is an isolated white d-pawn on d4 held back by a black e-pawn on e6. White's pawn has a dual nature. It can be weak because it's isolated, restrained, and subject to attack along the half-open d-file. This weakness is pronounced in the endgame, when it has little recourse and minimal dynamic compensation.

On the other side of the coin, the isolated d-pawn can also be strong because it is usually more advanced than the pawn restraining it, and therefore White gets a spatial edge that could translate into attack. Moreover, the isolated d-pawn serves as an excellent anchor for a white knight at e5 (sometimes c5). If Black were to try to keep White's pieces (mainly a knight) out of e5 by playing the f-pawn to f6, the e-pawn would be weakened. This weakened e-pawn would then be vulnerable along the e-file and possibly the a2-e6 diagonal. Furthermore, if White can advance the d-pawn in a timely way, the resulting exchanges might lead to greater freedom for White's pieces in the center.

Everything depends on which isolated d-pawn shows up: the weak one or the strong one. If you have an isolated d-pawn, make it strong. If you are playing against one, make it weak. The good player takes either side of the bet and wins.

299 □ What is a blockade?

According to Aron Nimzovich, a blockade is a "mechanical obstruction of an enemy pawn by a piece." Nimzovich, one of the pioneers of modern chess theory, first defined the concept of blockade in a 1924 treatise by the same name. Although any pawn may fall under a blockade, the strategy is most wisely employed against both passed and isolated pawns.

300 □ When should I blockade an enemy pawn?

Consider blockading your opponent's pawns when it's beneficial to prevent their movement. Blockade passed pawns to stop their march toward promotion. Blockade enemy isolated pawns to impede the action of their own pieces, leaving them cramped, less mobile, and passive. Starve, crush, and kill.

301 □ When are blockades possible?

Blockades can happen if there are no pawns on adjacent files to drive away the blockader. Since an isolated pawn has no friendly pawns on either side of it for support, it can easily fall victim to an immobilizing blockade. Passed pawns often go solo, also without a supportive partner to the right or left, and therefore can be blockaded too. But sometimes, whether isolated or passed, the blockaded pawn is joined by a friendly pawn (because of an exchange), and the two become assailants to break the blockade.

302 □ Which are the most effective and least effective blockaders?

Knights are generally the most effective blockaders. They can sit unassailably in front of an isolated pawn while attacking at full power. Moreover, if the blockading knight is protected, it doesn't have to retreat from an enemy piece attack, for no piece is weaker in value. (A protected blockader has to retreat only if it's more valuable than the piece that threatens it or if tactics necessitate it.)

The least effective blockader is usually a rook. Even when protected, it can be driven away by a diagonal bishop attack or by a knight attack, since either piece is less valuable than the rook (surrendering the rook for a bishop or a knight means the loss of two exchange points in relative value). The rook's blockading value is also reduced in rook-and-pawn endings when no minor pieces are on the board, because it's still vulnerable to a diagonal attack from the enemy king.

Surprisingly, the king can be an excellent blockader in many endgame situations. The queen can be a good blockader too, but using it carries the drawback of restricting the most powerful piece to passivity.

DOUBLE DOUBLE TOIL AND TROUBLE
303 □ What are doubled pawns?

Doubled pawns are two pawns that belong to one player and occupy the same file. They occur when a pawn moves over to a neighboring file by capturing or recapturing.

Doubled pawns should generally be avoided, but there are times (for example, if you need to open lines for attack) when accepting them gains other advantages. They certainly shouldn't be avoided if it means neglecting other relevant factors.

304 □ What are isolated doubled pawns?

Isolated doubled pawns are doubled pawns that can't be defended by other pawns because there are no friendly pawns on adjacent files. If they're subject to attack, especially from along a half-open file in front of them, they can be quite difficult to uphold. Avoid them if you can.

305 □ When are doubled pawns weak?

Doubled pawns can be weak for several reasons: (1) as a group they tend to crawl along (the back one can't move until the front one does), so they often obstruct the development of their own forces; (2) their movement can be frustrated by a single enemy pawn, either by blocking them on the same file or, from an adjacent file, by guarding a square they need to pass over; (3) the exchange producing them might also result in the creation of an isolated pawn; and (4) they might be isolated themselves, so that neither can be defended by a pawn and therefore one or both may be subject to direct piece attack. But they're not weak if they can't be exploited, and what doesn't kill us makes us strong.

306 □ When should I be willing to accept doubled pawns?

You may accept doubled pawns to: (1) open lines for attack; (2) facilitate or expedite development; (3) add protection to key squares; (4) bulwark a castled king's position; (5) create an escape square for the king; (6) save time if it would be wasted trying to avoid doubled pawns; (7) simplify the position; (8) win material; (9) avoid material loss; and/or (10) make necessary captures or recaptures.

307 □ If I must accept doubled pawns by capturing or recapturing with either a wing pawn or a pawn closer to the center, which pawn should I use for capturing?

This often difficult decision is subject to the given position's subtleties. As a rough guide, capture toward the center (with a wing pawn) so you have a greater chance to control the center. It discourages the enemy from occupying squares in that region.

But this also has drawbacks. Don't: (1) create an unfavorable pawn imbalance, allowing your opponent to manufacture a dangerous passed pawn; (2) miss out on your own opportunity to produce a passed pawn; (3) spawn a weak and exploitable isolated pawn, reducing your own forces to passivity; (4) expose your castled king's position to enemy assault; and/or (5) enable your opponent to prevent castling on one wing altogether.

Even so, it is preferable to capture toward the center if the resulting advantages outweigh the disadvantages.

308 □ Strictly speaking, should I avoid doubled pawns or accept them?

Avoid them if you can, but keep in mind the exceptions.

Chess instructors often have a problem teaching students about doubled pawns. They want to alert a student to their inherent drawbacks but not influence the student to avoid them automatically. This could lead to bad positions and lost games.

One example is when a student's opponent captures a piece with a piece and the student fails to take back because it would result in doubled pawns. It's usually much worse to be a piece down with healthy pawns than to be materially even with doubled pawns.

The same kind of bad reasoning prevails when a student fails to take back because it would expose the king or lead to loss of the castling privilege. If there is no obvious way to exploit your king's exposed position or its inability thereafter to castle, you should take back. To be a piece down is usually worse than being unable to castle, but it's your decision.

309 □ If I'm playing White, with a pawn on e4 facing a black pawn on e5, and my opponent has a bishop on c5, attacking along the a7-f2 diagonal with an eye on my f2-pawn, should I avoid offering a bishop trade on e3 if I would have to take back with the f2-pawn, doubling my e-pawns?

This is often a promising exchange for White and a poor one for Black. Though it doubles White's pawns on the e-file, they are usually good doubled pawns. The pawn on e4 guards d5 and f5, while the new pawn on e3 keeps Black pieces out of d4 and f4. You would thereby control more of the center than your opponent.

Moreover, you could then use the f-file to activate your king-rook, preferably by castling kingside. And your queen could be developed by shifting to e1, where it could enter the fray along the e1-h4 diagonal, an option it doesn't have with the f-pawn on f2.

In most cases you will find that the white pawn complex c2, d3, e4, and e3 has tremendous vitality and should not be avoided. If there are any potential drawbacks, it would be the pawn at e3, which could be attacked. Another weakness might be the a7-g1 diagonal.

But usually these weaknesses are overshadowed by the latent power of White's altered pawn state and the useful opening of the f-file and the e1-h4 diagonal. (The same kinds of advantages would redound to Black if a white bishop posted on c4 could take on e6, doubling Black's e-pawns.)

310 □ **I**f Black shouldn't double White's e-pawns by exchanging bishops on e3, as in the previous question, what should be done instead?

If it seems that White will gain the overall advantage from the exchange on e3, Black could do one of the following, if possible: (1) block the attack on the c5-bishop by putting the c6-knight in the way at d4, so that if an exchange takes place on d4, Black can take back with the c5-bishop or the e5-pawn (especially effective if a white knight occupies c3, obstructing the c-pawn's advance to c3 to guard d4); (2) retreat the bishop to b6, and if White captures there, Black takes back with the a-pawn, opening the a-file for the queen-rook; (3) protect the bishop with the queen at e7, so that if an exchange takes place on c5, the bishop is replaced by the queen; (4) defend the bishop by moving the d-pawn to d6, so that if a c5-exchange takes place, Black will have a half-open d-file and two pawns (c5 and e5) in position to control d4 (which is okay, provided neither the c5-pawn nor e5-pawn is meaningfully endangered); (5) ignore the attack to the bishop if it is already defended by the d-pawn, the queen, or the b-pawn; and (6) move it to b4, pinning the c3-knight.

By the same reasoning, White would have similar options if the c4-bishop were opposed by Black's e6-bishop.

311 □ **H**ow should I play against my opponent's doubled pawns?

You should try to: (1) prevent their movement by guarding, preferably with a pawn, the square immediately in front of them; (2) attack the doubled pawns and utilize the weak squares around them; (3) reduce any possible counterplay by productive piece exchanges; (4) mobilize your own pawn majority, if you have one, to create a passed pawn; and (5) avoid trades that would repair your opponent's pawn structure.

312 □ How should I play if I'm beset with doubled pawns?

If you have doubled pawns: (1) resist moving the front pawn unless you can exchange it for a healthy enemy pawn; (2) move the front one if it will not be in danger and will prevent enemy pawns from safely advancing; (3) utilize the open lines for development, especially by placing a rook on the open file created as a result of obtaining doubled pawns; and (4) avoid piece exchanges that reduce activity and accentuate the doubled pawns' inherent weaknesses. Be good to them and they'll be good to you.

313 □ If I have a doubled pawn, how should I undouble it?

If you can do so safely, advance it to bring about an exchange of pawns: your doubled pawn for your opponent's healthy one.

Don't seek to exchange it, however, if there's some tactical reason to retain it. For example, don't move the doubled pawn if it provides needed shelter or guards important squares. And don't worry unduly about doubled-pawn weaknesses if other concerns, such as your opponent's immediate mate threats, are more pressing.

HANGING BACKWARD AND ISOLATED

314 □ What is a backward pawn?

A pawn whose neighboring pawns are too far advanced to protect it is backward. Without protection, it can't safely advance. Moreover, the square immediately in front of it is usually controlled by an enemy pawn, and the enemy's major pieces have access to (and may already occupy) the half-open file in front of it.

In fact, the square in front of the backward pawn, dominated by the enemy, can function as a fortuitous outpost for an enemy knight, for no pawn can guard that square to keep the knight out.

Backward pawns are debilitating weaknesses, often engendering passivity and a lack of space for the defender. Avoid them.

315 □ How should I play against a backward pawn?

To exploit a backward pawn: (1) thoroughly control, with at least one pawn and several pieces, the square immediately in front of it; (2) obstruct its advance by occupying the square in front of it with a piece, preferably a knight; (3) counter every enemy piece attack on your obstructing piece with a piece defense of your own, so if you must recapture, you can do so with a piece; (4) pile up on the backward pawn with rooks and queen along the half-open file it occupies; (5) avoid exchanges that reduce the pressure against it; (6) seek exchanges that make it harder to defend; (7) avoid recapturing on the square immediately in front of it with a pawn, for then your own pawn will obstruct your major pieces from attacking the backward pawn frontally; and (8) watch for tactics that allow your opponent to advance and dissolve it.

Generally, maintain the pressure on a backward pawn until your opponent runs out of options and makes a mistake.

316 □ What are hanging pawns?

Hanging pawns are two pawns of the same color on adjacent files occupying their fourth rank. Both are subject to enemy rook and queen attack along half-open files in front of them. The squares to which either pawn might advance are guarded (or can be guarded) by enemy pawns, so that the hanging pawns are restrained. To avoid this inhibiting effect, it's sometimes desirable to advance one or both of the pawns, preventing or dissuading the enemy pawns from establishing restraint. Hanging pawns can be either favorable or unfavorable, depending on the specifics of the position.

317 □ When are hanging pawns weak and when are they strong?

Hanging pawns become weak when the enemy can guard the squares in front of them with pawns and pieces, restraining their advance while subjecting them to attack, especially frontally along the half-open files. If the hanging pawns then advance, even with adequate protection, they could incur other weaknesses that worsen the situation. Eventually, material might be lost.

However, hanging pawns can often bring an advantage in space. They can also be strong because they guard a block of four consecutive squares on the rank in front of them, preventing enemy pieces from utilizing those squares. Moreover, they have the potential to advance. If an exchange of pawns takes place, the adjacent hanging pawn could take back, producing a passed pawn. Properly supported, that pawn could become a threat to advance and promote. Generally, hanging pawns can tie up the enemy, for considerable effort may have to be expended to watch out for their possible advances.

It depends which side of the wager you take. Try to support the advance of your own hanging pawns to gain attacking chances. When playing against them, try to restrain their advance and undermine them.

318 □ What is an isolated pawn pair?

Sometimes called a couplet or couple, an isolated pawn pair consists of two friendly pawns on half-open files connected diagonally, so that the back one, which has advanced one square, defends the front one, which has advanced two squares. Both pawns are restrained from advancing further because the squares immediately in front of them are controlled by enemy pawns and pieces. If they advance they'll be captured and won. Usually they can be attacked by enemy rooks and queen on the half-open files in front of them.

The isolated pawn couple can be weak for three reasons: (1) the couple's back pawn can't be protected by a pawn and is therefore quite vulnerable; (2) the squares in front of the pawns make ideal resting spots for enemy pieces, since there are no pawns on adjacent files to guard those squares; and (3) the side having them tends to get a cramped, lifeless, defensive game, with little scope for activity.

If you are playing against the isolated pawn couple, try to utilize the weak squares by occupying the strong points and discouraging enemy counterplay. If you are hampered by this weak complex, try to develop counterplay elsewhere, pulling off enemy resources and denying your opponent the time to operate against the weaknesses. And if you can get rid of them by suddenly advancing and trading them for good pawns, do so.

THE ANALYTIC METHOD

319 □ What is the analytic method in chess?

The analytic method is a question and answer process to elicit information that will help you select your next move. You silently ask yourself exploratory questions about the position. The information generated helps you decide how to respond to enemy threats and to pursue your own aims, enabling you to evaluate the position and settle on a move that meets all your needs.

After you've grown accustomed to this self-questioning, you will automatically look for answers without having to be cued. But this won't happen overnight. You'll need a lot of deliberate practice actually thinking and formulating these questions before the process becomes automatic.

320 □ What must I do before forming a plan of action?

Before forming a plan, you must evaluate the position. By enumerating each side's pluses and minuses, considering static features first and then dynamic ones, you'll determine who stands better and why. Then you can attempt to conceive a plan that capitalizes on your strengths while minimizing your weaknesses.

Begin by making a mental list of your strong suits. Note the well-posted pieces, the key lines of attack you control, and any effective pawn majorities you possess, and see if any pawn advances seem inviting, for example.

Then make a similar list of your weaknesses. Do you have defensible squares and pawns? Is your king's position endangered? Are your pieces constricted or ineffective? And so on.

After evaluating your side, run the same analysis on the enemy's position (if time permits). When you have finished comparing assets and liabilities, you'll be ready to plot a rational course of action.

If a position is relatively balanced, both sides will have offsetting advantages and disadvantages. Steinitz, the first world champion, initially espoused the theory that to gain one kind of advantage you had to surrender another kind of comparable worth. Plainly, you don't get something for nothing—the principal principle of positional chess.

321 □ What are the main objectives of a plan?

A reasonable plan attempts to do one or more of the following: (1) exploit enemy weaknesses; (2) remove or lessen enemy strengths; (3) eliminate or ameliorate your own weaknesses; (4) build and capitalize on your own strengths. (Sounds like an ethic for the "me generation," doesn't it?)

322 □ What questions should I ask myself about my opponent's last move?

When reviewing your opponent's last move, ask yourself simple, direct questions. For example: (1) Does my opponent's last move threaten anything? (2) Does it respond adequately to my previous move? (3) Does it give me new opportunities? (4) Does it pose any future problems? (5) Can it be ignored? If you ask these and other related questions, at least your thinking will be germane.

323 □ If my response seems necessary or forced, should I waste time asking myself a series of questions?

If you're quite sure about the move being forced, and if you're playing with a clock, there's no need for an elaborate Q & A process. But before responding, make one last check to see if you've missed something obvious. In chess, it doesn't hurt to think, it hurts to lose.

324 □ How does an open game differ from a closed game?

In open games, the center is not blocked by pawns and events tend to happen quickly. They feature rapid development, play in the center, and coordinated attacks with many pieces. King safety is paramount.

Since closed games usually have blocked centers, they proceed at a much slower pace. Not much can happen in or through the center, and expeditious piece development is slightly less important. Also, king safety isn't usually a factor early on, so quick castling may not be necessary. In fact, you might not castle at all.

Many principles that apply to open games are modified in closed games. For example, in open games you worry about placing knights on the edge of the board or bringing out the queen too early. In closed games, however, there may be many opportunities to violate these principles to good effect, depending on the situation. Be opportunistic.

325 □ What does it mean to accumulate small advantages?

This is a modern theory of positional play. Without incurring risk, you try to gain many small advantages, step by step, until they add up to a very great advantage that leads to a mating attack or forces the opponent to surrender material. Rather than playing for a win or a draw, a positional player plays not to lose. The theory of positional play was put forth by Wilhelm Steinitz (1836–1900), the first official world champion, who held the title from 1886 to 1894.

Some leading players didn't understand or appreciate Steinitz's ideas. Describing Steinitz's play, the English master Henry Bird (1830–1908) once said: "Place the contents of the chessbox in your hat, shake them up vigorously, pour them on the board at a height of two feet, and you get the style of Steinitz."

326 □ What are small advantages?

Generally, small advantages are intangible strengths that are hard to measure and evaluate, compared with, say, being up a piece, which is a concrete advantage having a definite value. Control of an open file or diagonal, slightly better piece placement, slightly more space, a good minor piece opposing a bad one, fewer pawn weaknesses, a slightly safer king's position—all are typical small advantages.

327 □ Why should I bother to add protection to something that's already guarded?

How well have you analyzed? Perhaps something you think is already protected isn't, so overzealousness is a kind of insurance. The protection you already have can suddenly be undermined by exchanges, checks, and other threats. Or you might want to relieve certain protectors for other duty, which means they must be replaced first (adding a single extra protector can free up any of the others).

Additional protectors also give you a choice of ways to take back when an enemy captures. Most important, this gives you the option in some positions of recapturing with a particular unit or type of unit. For example, you may want to recapture with a piece on a particular square so that you can continue using that square by replacing the captured piece with another piece. If you take back with a pawn instead, the square becomes relatively unusable because it's much harder to get a friendly pawn out of the way. It has no real mobility.

Finally, you might overprotect a particular square so that the enemy can't use it to clear space, especially by a sudden pawn advance. If you guard that square a number of times, an enemy pawn advance to it will probably result in loss of that pawn.

328 □ Is a weakness really so bad if I can adequately guard it?

To sufficiently protect or safeguard a weakness, you may have to make concessions that lead to other problems. For example, in defending it, your pieces could become passive and lack scope. Furthermore, defending a weakness ties down your overall game plan to some extent, for you have to wait for your opponent's strategy to materialize before you can follow through more fully on your own.

But the most serious drawback is that whenever you are constrained to defend one place, you almost necessarily weaken another. Fresh weaknesses such as this often prove to be the defender's downfall, especially with defending forces out of position and tied to the first trouble spot.

This explains the endgame principle of "two weaknesses": before proceeding with the final attack, first induce your opponent into incurring a second weakness, after which defense becomes difficult.

The message is clear: avoid unnecessary weaknesses.

329 □ What is the difference between a permanent advantage and a temporary one?

Permanent advantages are concrete and tangible. If you have such advantages at an early point in the game, you'll probably have them later on as well. They are clear and can be counted or seen.

Two examples of these lasting advantages are a material plus and a superior pawn structure. If you're ahead by a knight, you are likely to remain a knight ahead unless something radical happens to overturn the position. Material doesn't disappear by itself. And if your pawn structure is fluid, with no weaknesses, it's likely to remain so unless debilitating exchanges or advances take place, which don't happen by magic.

Temporary advantages are fleeting and intangible. You can't quite put your finger on them. If you don't immediately exploit them, you'll lose them. Time is an example of a temporary advantage. When you're ahead in development, if you don't utilize it soon your opponent will catch up. If you have the initiative, you must capitalize on it before the attack passes to your opponent.

In determining the overall superiority in a chess position, consider both tangible and intangible factors, how they interact and influence each other, and their contribution to a position's equilibrium.

330 □ How must I choose when faced with conflicting principles?

Consider the circumstances and you may be able to decide which of the two principles carries more weight in the given situation. In most cases, you'll actually have to decide without relying on chess platitudes or perfunctory wisdom. It's called thinking, and you have to do it in your head.

331 □ When is it desirable to assume a slight disadvantage in a position?

Suppose, for example, you know that a certain opening variation gives your opponent objectively better chances than you, but you also know that your opponent is uncomfortable in that line and has mishandled it in the past. If the variation doesn't lose perforce, and if you have some feeling for it, you can head right into it, especially if other circumstances such as your tournament standing apply.

Also, if you have some minor problems in a position, you'll probably work hard to alleviate them and avoid a worsened situation. On the other hand, your opponent, having the advantage, may tend to let up and make mistakes. It's possible to overextend oneself and lose by relying too much on the slight advantage. Or your opponent might play mechanically in looking for simplification, while you become resourceful as you try to survive. It's not always clear in those cases who really has the advantage.

332 □ What are some reasons for simplifying a position?

You simplify a position by exchanging pieces and sometimes pawns, and by avoiding unclear variations that are difficult to evaluate. Generally, players are advised to simplify to emphasize the advantage of a large material plus.

Other reasons to simplify are to: (1) force a draw, if you are losing or feel at risk; (2) lessen the force of your opponent's attack, especially when under heavy fire; (3) obtain a clear-cut position emphasizing your advantage while denying your opponent counterplay; and (4) establish a simplified, familiar type of position with which you feel at home.

Hear this proviso, though. If you find yourself in exchanging situations, don't automatically simplify. Make sure you first understand the position and the anticipated consequences of a series of trades before making them. If you like what you see, that's fine, go ahead and trade. But remember, once you've exchanged down, you can't go home again.

333 □ If I need to waste a move to gain time to think things over, is it advisable to move my castled king to the corner if it doesn't incur tactical problems?

If you're going to move your castled king to the corner, do it to avoid an immediate or upcoming tactical threat. Don't do it just to waste a move, because it could entail endgame difficulties.

This wasted move probably means it would take your king an extra turn to get to the center once the endgame starts, and that could let your opponent's king get to the center first, gaining superiority and forcing a winning invasion. Waste a move now and lose the game later.

If you need to waste a move, it's better to do so by improving the scope of one of your pieces, even if only slightly. Or, if you can, add some additional protection to a key point already sufficiently guarded.

334 □ Which is better, counterattack or pure defense?

Counterattack is more attractive than defense, so I can understand why it's preferred. Indeed, if you can combine defense with counterattack, you're in good shape.

But there are two potential problems: (1) You may become so concerned with counterattack that you forget to answer your opponent's threat. What good is it to threaten mate when you get mated yourself first? (2) You can meet with a sad end if, instead of responding to a small threat, you issue a threat of your own. If your opponent answers your own threat by creating an additional new one, you'll suddenly be faced with two threats yourself: the old one you ignored and the new one.

I recommend counterattack whenever it can be constructive, and if it meets the general requirements of the position. But sometimes you must simply defend and wait for glory another day.

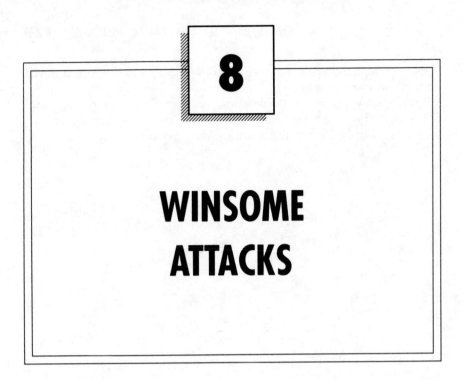

8

WINSOME ATTACKS

STRATEGY AND TACTICS; ATTACK AND DEFENSE; SIMPLE AND COMPLEX

335 □ What is the difference between strategy and tactics?

At the highest levels these concepts merge into an overall approach, but it's helpful to note the different philosophies they represent.

A strategy is a plan, and tactics are the individual operations needed to bring about that plan. Strategy is longterm, tactics immediate. Strategy is general, tactics are specific. For example, a strategy could be to attack the enemy's castled position. The tactics of this imaginary situation might be focused on the square g7, which in our scenario could be attacked as follows: (1) by transferring the queen-rook to the open b-file, lifting it to the third rank, and then moving it across to g3; (2) by maneuvering a knight to f5, perhaps from f3 to d4 to f5; (3) by flanking the queen-bishop from c1 to b2; and (4) by introducing the queen, moving it from d1 to g4.

Of course there are other methods of attempting to achieve the same kinds of attack, but the point is clear. These steps are separate, tactical parts of a greater, strategic idea.

336 □ When is a move considered forced?

Technically, a forced move is played when there is no other legal response. Usually, though, a forced move is the only reasonable move. Other moves are possible but are so bad or so illogical that they are beyond serious consideration. A forced move is often the only sensible move.

337 □ When is it a disadvantage to give a check?

Checks must be judged by the same criteria used for all other moves. A careless check may lead to trouble in several ways.

Suppose, instead of replying to an enemy threat, you choose to give a check. If your check is answered by a new threat to the checking piece, as is often the case, you suddenly face two threats instead of one. To avoid losing material, you'd have to answer both threats with one move.

Meaningless checking also loses time. When you give a bishop check, for example, and your opponent blocks with a supported pawn, attacking the bishop, your bishop is forced to move and you've probably wasted time.

Even if you don't lose time or material, you're wasting the opportunity to give that check later, when you might need it to save a piece or maintain your position or gain a tempo. Checking should never be a reflex move.

338 □ How does an attack differ from a threat?

These similar chess terms are often used synonymously. They are a little different, however, and though the terms apply to both material and nonmaterial targets, the difference may be more easily understood by considering captures.

You are attacking an enemy unit when one of your units is in position to capture it. But this attack isn't automatically a threat, for it's not always desirable to capture an enemy unit. Capturing for nothing, however, usually is.

If you are in line to capture a unit but the enemy has adequate protection for it, you are attacking, not threatening. If you are in line to capture and win material because the protection is inadequate, or to gain some other advantage, you are attacking and also threatening. It's a fine, albeit useful, distinction.

339 □ What's the main way to win material in chess?

Besides taking hanging units for nothing, you usually win material by giving some form of double attack. The double attacks that usually score tend to have a direct, or obvious component, as well as an indirect, or subtle component. It's more natural for the opponent (I'm assuming it's not Garry Kasparov) to focus on the overt threat while missing or failing to appreciate the deceptive one.

DISCOVERING PINS, SKEWERS, AND FORKS

340 □ What is a pin?

A pin is a tactic that prevents or discourages an enemy unit from moving off the line of attack, because to do so would expose another unit to capture or a key square to occupation.

There are usually three chess units involved in a pin: (1) the pinned unit, (2) the screened unit (or square), and (3) the pinning (or attacking) piece.

341 □ What's the difference between a relative and an absolute pin?

A relative pin is one in which the pinned unit is pinned to anything other than the king. The pinned unit can be moved, though that could bring disaster. An absolute pin is one in which the pinned unit is pinned to its king. The pinned unit can't move off the line of attack, for it's illegal to expose the king to capture.

342 □ What's the advantage of a pin?

The pinned unit is immobilized, severely hampering its functioning. And if the pin is absolute, the victim is unable to move off the line of attack. Moreover, there may be no need to capture a pinned unit at once. Instead, because of its helplessness, you may have a chance to pile up on it, attacking it again and again, preferably with pawns and minor pieces, until a material advantage can be realized. In chess, the strong exploit the weak.

343 □ Can a pinned piece give check?

Many players are confused over this, thinking that once a piece is pinned, it's not allowed to give check or its check can be ignored. This is simply not so.

A typical occurrence is to block a check with a piece that thereby gives a check itself. Even though the blocking piece is pinned to its king, it still gives check to the opponent's king.

A check is a check, even when delivered by a pinned unit. Respect it or pay.

344 □ How can I defend myself once I've been pinned?

The best defense is to avoid getting pinned. But if you do get pinned, you can defend by: (1) interposing a defender between the pinned unit and the pinner; (2) adding protection to the pinned unit, especially if the added defender is of small value; (3) moving the target (the unit to which the victim unit is pinned), if you can do so with a gain of time or in a way that avoids loss of the pinned unit; (4) moving the pinned unit off the line of attack (this works only if it's a relative pin and when you are willing to accept the consequences); (5) moving the pinned unit along the line of the pinner to capture it if both units are of like power; and (6) driving or luring away the pinner, if possible, ending the pin.

345 □ What is "putting the question to the bishop"?

Usually, this is an attempt to end a pin on a knight. You "put the question to the bishop" when you try to drive away a bishop by a pawn attack, generally by moving a rook-pawn.

Suppose, for example, as White, you have a bishop on g5 that pins a black knight on f6 to the black queen on d8. If Black can safely play the h-pawn from h7 to h6, White's bishop will either have to withdraw (to h4 or toward c1) or capture the knight. By putting the question to the bishop (attacking the bishop with the h-pawn), Black forces White to commit to a definite course of action, either an exchange or a retreat. Putting the question to the bishop asks, Are you going to capture my knight, retreat but keep the pin, or move away?

346 □ Suppose my opponent retreats the bishop to h4 in the previous situation. Should I then break the pin on my knight by advancing the g-pawn two squares?

The unpinning of the knight requires careful consideration. Of course, Black would like to end the tension caused by the pin, but the two-square advance of the g-pawn may pose certain problems. If castled kingside, you should avoid the pin-breaking advance (g7 to g5) when: (1) the resulting weaknesses on h6, h5, and f5 are severe and exploitable; (2) the g-pawn would be rendered an obvious target for attack (subject to the flanking advance, h2 to h4, for example); and (3) the f3-knight can be sacrificed on g5 for two pawns, a maintenance of the bishop pin, and a wide open kingside attack. If all this militates against the g-pawn's advance, you may simply have to bite the bullet, accept the condition of your knight, and keep up its adequate protection.

347 □ Is a pin useful when it doesn't force a gain of material?

Some pins are valuable simply because they restrict the enemy's options by preventing or discouraging pieces from moving. They may also result in the enemy's loss of time, especially if effort must be made to protect the pinned unit or extricate it from the pin.

Pawn moves that attack or attempt to drive off the pinning piece (like "putting the question to the bishop") invariably have strategic consequences. The resulting changes in pawn formation usually leave weak squares and provide targets for new attacks.

348 □ What is a skewer?

A skewer is the reverse of a pin—a straight-line tactic by which a friendly piece attacks two enemy units along the same rank, file, or diagonal; the more valuable front unit is compelled to move, exposing the less valuable back one to capture.

This differs from a pin, where the less valuable front enemy unit (the one under immediate attack) shields the more valuable second unit (the one in back) from capture, and therefore can't or shouldn't move.

349 □ If both enemy units under straight-line attack are the same kind of piece, how can you tell if the tactic is a pin or skewer?

It has to do with the enemy unit in front. When it can't or shouldn't move, then it's a pin. But when it must or should move, then it's a skewer. The same logic works when the attacked enemy units are a bishop and knight—different in power, but similar in value. If the front piece is frozen, it's a pin; if it's being chased, it's a skewer.

350 □ What is a discovery?

Also called a discovered attack, a discovery is another straight-line tactic. But instead of one unit victimizing two enemy units on the same line, it's an attack by two friendly units against one or more enemy units. You give a discovery by moving a unit off a rank, file, or diagonal, unveiling an attack against an enemy unit by a stationary friendly piece that was formerly shielded by the moving unit. Meanwhile, the moving unit can also threaten or attack an enemy unit.

If the stationary attacker gives check, it's called a discovered check. If both the moving and stationary attackers give check, it's called double check, a very powerful move, even for chess.

351 □ When are discoveries most menacing?

Discoveries are sneaky tactics, and almost always have surprise value. They assume greater potency when the moving unit also attacks, thereby posing two threats with one move. The real sting may actually come from the moving unit, which often has carte blanche to threaten or capture with impunity, since the enemy must respond to the discovered check first.

352 □ What is the most common double attack?

It's called a fork. This is a tactic by which a unit attacks two or more enemy units on the same move. Every kind of unit can give a fork.

The queen can give the most forks, since it can strike in all directions. But the pawn perhaps gives the most serious forks. Whatever it attacks, it can capture without loss of material, even if it's something already protected, because nothing is less valuable than a pawn.

353 □ What kind of fork is the most difficult to answer?

The knight fork can be really tough. No other unit moves like a knight except another knight, so it has more opportunities to fork without fear of being captured by the units it is forking.

Particularly memorable are triple attacks called royal forks or family forks. On the same move, a knight attacks the enemy king, queen, and rook, none of which is able to defend by capturing the knight. The squares c2 and c7 are focal points for many family forks. For example, a white knight moving to or capturing on c7 often can simultaneously check an uncastled king at e8, attack an unmoved rook at a8, and attack a black queen that has been lured to b5, d5, or e6.

354 □ What's the tactic known as undermining?

The concept of undermining is perhaps better understood when we refer to its other names: removing the guard and removing the defender. You undermine a piece when you capture or drive away its protection. Frequently, underminings are tied in with other tactics, such as pins. For example, when a bishop pins a knight, the idea may not be to win the knight but to undermine the knight's protection of another unit. It's insidious.

355 □ Which tactics occur most often?

By far the two most frequently occurring tactics are forks and pins. They arise in practically every game. Three other common tactics are skewers, discoveries, and underminings. These five weapons generally constitute the major nonmating tactics (those mainly concerned with winning material).

MORE TACTICS

356 □ What is a multiple threat?

When you make two or more independent threats on the same turn, you're giving a multiple threat. A multiple threat could be as simple as a straightforward fork, or as complex as a combination of tactical themes, like developing a bishop off the front rank to attack an undefended knight while simultaneously clearing a path for a rook shift to threaten mate. The threats are different in nature, but stem from the same move, a multiple threat.

357 □ What is a combination?

There is no universally accepted definition for a combination. The basic disagreement centers on whether it requires sacrifice. In this book we'll say a combination is a forcing variation with a sacrifice. It pursues a positive aim and leads to a qualitative change in the position. In other words, it's a good thing to do.

358 □ How should I study tactics?

There are many effective approaches to studying tactics. The following are tactics I recommend you practice: (1) direct captures, first with only necessary material present, then in more complex situations; (2) simple checkmates, in which the material is arranged by pattern or theme, with the diagrams showing only necessary units; (3) simple nonmating tactics, defining and illustrating forks, pins, skewers, discoveries, and underminings; (4) deeper tactics and combinations, mating and nonmating, in which the tactics are still arranged thematically; (5) random deep problems, with no particular arrangement, where any theme is possible, as in real chess; (6) a steady diet of speed and practice games in which the student must play tactically and sacrificially, regardless of the situation and stylistic preferences; (7) the study of brilliancies and complex attacking games of the great masters, demonstrating how, at the highest levels, tactics and strategy merge.

359 □ When pursuing the study of tactics, do I have to do it all in my head, or is it all right to move the pieces on a board?

In my opinion, if you want to improve quickly and to the fullest, analyze in your head every chance you get.

360 □ Is there a trick I could use to help me solve tactical problems?

There are many things you can try, but if I had to give one piece of advice, it would be to reverse the move order. It's not unusual to get the right idea but in the wrong order of moves. Instead of abandoning the idea when you don't see that it leads anywhere, turn it around. That is, try the second move first.

You'd be surprised how often this works. The reason we don't do this automatically is that the second move is frequently more violent and may entail sacrifice. Naturally, to avoid sacrifice, we look for a move of preparation. But reality doesn't wait—it's gone with the next move.

9

STAR'S END

THE EASY STUFF

361 □ **W**hy should I study the endgame if I never get into the endgame?

There is much to be learned from endgame study, such as an understanding of the raw powers of the pieces. This information has application throughout an entire game of chess. The reason you never get to the endgame may be that you've never studied it and fear it, so you shy away from it.

362 □ **W**hat are the chief characteristics of the endgame?

Endgames are distinguishable from openings and middlegames in at least several of the following ways: (1) fewer pieces are on the board (often the queens have been exchanged); (2) the kings are more active;

(3) calculations can be more precise; (4) the relative values of the units change (pawns become more important and minor pieces less important); (5) material advantages are emphasized; and (6) it's often desirable not to move (because of *zugzwang* or the opposition).

363 □ Why should I safeguard my king in the opening but activate it in the endgame?

In the opening, you usually have to castle to get your king behind a wall of pawns. If not, your king can be subjected to a fierce assault from numerous enemy attackers, since the center is open (or may suddenly become so). But in the endgame, many of the enemy pieces (especially the queen) have been exchanged off the board, and the chance that a quick mating attack will sink your king is greatly reduced. Thus the benefits of using your king for attack and defense tend to outweigh the accompanying risk.

364 □ What is the foundation of most endgame theory?

Endgame theory is based on the conversion of an extra pawn into a win. Surely there are other factors that apply, such as basic mates, strengths and weaknesses of pieces, time, and so on. In numerous theoretical and practical endgames, moreover, one side may have a material advantage greater than a single pawn.

But the core of endgame theory has to be the methods and techniques for creating a passed pawn and advancing it to the promotion square, either to make a new queen or to force the defender into sacrificing a piece to stop the promotion. The extra piece will lead to a quick mate, win more enemy material, or help promote yet another pawn that will lead to mate.

365 □ Why are unmoved pawns often considered strong in the endgame?

Sometimes unmoved pawns are easier to defend and, having remained on their original squares, have created no pawn weaknesses. But the chief value of an unmoved pawn is that it's still capable of moving either one or two squares, which can be a critical option at the right moment.

366 □ What is a theoretical draw?

A theoretical draw is a position that well-documented theory proves should end in a draw if both sides play the best possible moves. So what? Chess is full of surprises. In your own games, when analyzing your opponent's possible future moves, always assume the best possible response. But be on the lookout for mistakes and be ready to exploit the pitfalls that lure an unwary victim.

367 □ How do I attempt to stop the advance of an enemy passed pawn in the endgame?

You can try to thwart the menace of an enemy passed pawn by: (1) controlling key squares in the pawn's path so it can't safely advance; (2) occupying a square in the pawn's path with a piece, called a blockade, that obstructs its advance; or (3) counterattacking seriously elsewhere, forcing defensive moves that deny the enemy the free hand needed to push the pawn.

As the attacker, when the enemy is tying up resources to stop your passed pawn's advance, try to open a second front on the other side, particularly by creating another passed pawn. To accomplish this, you may need to sacrifice a pawn or two, but it's often worth it. In chess, the end often does justify the means.

368 □ How can I determine whether my king can catch up with a passed pawn, preventing it from safely promoting?

There are two things you can do in this case. One is to count the number of moves it takes for the pawn to promote, and the number it takes your king to reach the queening square. If the numbers are the same, the king overtakes the pawn. If the pawn needs fewer moves, it queens.

Another method is to visualize the "square of the pawn." If the defending king can move within the square of the pawn, it stops the pawn; if not, the pawn promotes.

369 □ What is the "square of the pawn"?

The "square of the pawn" is a visual gimmick by which you can determine by merely looking, without calculation, whether a pawn can outrun the enemy king to the promotion square.

Rather than referring to a single square, however, the term signifies a box of squares forming a quadrangle, consisting of four, nine, sixteen, twenty-five, or thirty-six ordinary chessboard squares, representing quadrangles of two-by-two, three-by-three, four-by-four, five-by-five, and six-by-six squares respectively. The less advanced the pawn at the start, the bigger the quadrangle.

To see the quadrangle in your mind, draw a mental line from the square the pawn occupies to the promotion square. That line forms one of the four sides of an imagined quadrangle, extending in the direction of the enemy king.

Thus, if a white pawn occupies b5, the quadrangle runs from b5 to b8 to e8 to e5 to b5, and consists of a total of sixteen squares. If the black king (let's put it on f4 at the start) can move within that quadrangle (occupy any of those sixteen squares) on the immediate move, the pawn can be stopped. If the king can't enter the quadrangle, the pawn queens. In this example, Black to move catches the pawn by moving to e5; White to move wins by advancing to b6.

Practice "seeing" the square of the pawn as often as you can and you'll soon be able to make this determination instantly, enriching your game in unimagined ways.

370 □ Why is it important to know the ending of king and pawn vs. king?

In a sense, the king-and-pawn vs. king ending is the most important of all because every other ending can reduce to it. Even in difficult endgames, you'll need to consider whether it's desirable to exchange pieces, achieving this situation, which in its stark simplicity can actually be quite complex. Don't take it lightly.

371 □ How can a king and a pawn beat a lone king?

The pawn must promote to a queen or a rook in either of two ways: (1) the pawn advances to promotion without the need of support because the enemy king is too far away to catch it; or (2) the friendly king escorts the pawn to promotion, occupying and guarding key squares and preventing the enemy king from setting up a blockade.

372 □ What are the objectives for each side in king-and-pawn vs. king endings?

The side with the pawn wants to advance it and promote it to a queen, creating a king-and-queen vs. king ending, a basic mate that is fairly easy to win. The defender's objectives are: (1) to track down and take the pawn if it's undefended and separated from its king; (2) to blockade the pawn if it can be defended; or (3) in the event the pawn queens, to lure the attacking queen and king into setting up a stalemate blunder in the corner or along the board's edge.

373 □ What is a turning maneuver?

A turning maneuver is an outflanking stratagem by which the attacking king advances to reach important squares in front of its pawn. It occurs when the two kings stand face to face on the same file (or on the same rank), with one square separating them along a straight line. The defender, on move, must give ground to the left or right. If the first king goes right, the second advances on the left. If the first king goes left, the second moves right. Either way, the defender gets outflanked.

OUTFLANKING

374 □ When I have a king and a pawn and my opponent has only a king, should I advance my pawn first or my king?

If the pawn can queen by force, don't even think about it, push the pawn. But when the enemy king can block the pawn's advance, move your king instead. You're going to have to clear a path for the pawn anyway; if you advance your pawn precipitately, you move the critical squares farther up the board and generally make winning more difficult.

375 □ What is a squeeze?

A squeeze is a method whereby the attacking side is able to push the defending king off the queening square to assume control.

A typical squeeze situation for a knight-pawn, bishop-pawn, or center pawn begins this way: (1) the defending king occupies the queening square; (2) the pawn is on its sixth rank; and (3) the attacking king sits on the same sixth rank as the pawn on an adjacent file. The attacking king is therefore a knight's jump away from the queening square (if it were a knight, it actually could move to the queening square).

The squeeze results by advancing the pawn to the seventh rank without check. The defending king then has only one safe square, quitting the queening square and exiting to the side of the pawn. The attacking king then plows to the seventh rank, suddenly guarding the queening square and insuring the pawn's promotion.

376 □ Does the squeeze technique work for rook-pawns?

Rook-pawns can't squeeze. When you advance the pawn to the seventh rank, trying to squeeze out the enemy king, you stalemate because the enemy king doesn't have a safe square to the pawn's side. There's only the board's edge and deep space. Rook-pawns can only draw once the enemy king occupies the promotion square.

377 □ Is there a clue to whether you can play a successful squeeze?

As a rule of thumb, the squeeze works if you can advance a pawn to the seventh rank without giving check (and if it's not a rook-pawn). If not, the advance results in stalemate or the surrender of the pawn. The latter is also a draw because of insufficient mating material.

CRITICAL THINKING ON CRITICAL SQUARES

378 □ Do pawns other than rook-pawns present problems for the superior side in king-and-pawn vs. king endgames?

Sometimes a knight-pawn can pose a problem, for here, too, the edge of the board affords the defender occasional stalemate hopes. Correct play, however, can avert pitfalls and force a win.

If you have the option, simply advance your own king to rook-seven, preventing your opponent from using the corner for a drawing refuge. Let the defending king have access to the middle of the board instead, where there's no stalemate and plenty of space, the final frontier.

379 □ Can I force a win in king-and-rook-pawn vs. king situations by preventing the defending king from occupying the promotion square?

If your pawn can't be menaced, you win if your king can first occupy the knight-seven square or the knight-eight square on the file adjacent to the rook-pawn. This sets up a barrier thwarting the defending king's attempt to get in front of the pawn.

You can also win if, before the enemy king has crossed to the queening square, your own king occupies the adjacent knight-six square and your rook-pawn can advance to the seventh rank without check, creating an impenetrable fortress.

Moving your king in front of your rook-pawn to keep the enemy king out of the corner won't necessarily win. The enemy king may trap your own king against the board's edge, impeding the pawn's advance and insuring a draw.

380 □ Is it difficult to win with an extra rook-pawn, the only pawn on the board, in endings with other pieces (not just kings) also on the board?

Generally, yes, though it depends. The problem is that the rook-pawn is at the board's edge. This tends to reduce the attacker's options, since play only takes place on one side of the pawn.

The defender's resources are less burdened because the play must take place in a restricted sector of the board. Often a purely passive defense will suffice to hold the position, even though in many defensive cases a good counter is considered the best defense. But against an extra rook-pawn, the defending king (and sometimes other pieces) frequently finds safety entrenched in front of the pawn or even on the promotion square, where it can't be driven out. Finally, the defender's stalemate possibilities are greatly increased when confronting a rook-pawn.

The ending of king, bishop, and rook-pawn vs. king, where the bishop lacks the ability to control the promotion square, is a flagrant example. Once the defender's king establishes itself on the queening square, there's no way to win or force it out.

HOLDING THE FORTRESS

381 □ Is it ever advantageous to have an extra rook-pawn?

Any kind of extra pawn is generally useful. But rook-pawns tend to be less valuable than other pawns, with some exceptions. They might be desirable in: (1) certain minor-piece endings, where the pawn's proximity to the edge reduces the defensive piece's mobility (the piece runs out of places to move); and (2) king-and-pawn endings, where a distant rook-pawn can be used as a decoy to lure the enemy king away so the main body of pawns, lying on the other flank, can be fleeced by the attacking king.

382 □ What is a critical square?

A critical square is one that is occupied by the superior king to enable it to insure the success of a task. In some endings, the attacker's occupation of a critical square enables the win to be forced. In other instances, occupying a critical square might only lead to the gain of material with winning chances. To exploit a critical square, the attacker's king must occupy it. To stop the exploitation of a critical square, the defender's king must guard it. Rather than occupying a critical square, a defending king simply has to prevent the attacking king from doing so.

383 □ Why doesn't occupying a critical square by the superior king always lead to victory?

In king-and-pawn vs. king endings, the attacker can win by force when the king occupies the pawn's critical squares. The defender tries to avert this to be able to draw. With more pawns on the board, however, occupation of a critical square won't necessarily lead to a forced win, though this depends on the specific situation.

For example, it may simply win a pawn, which doesn't assure victory in itself. The defender may still be able to frustrate the attacker's attempt at promoting the extra pawn by seizing a meaningful opposition.

384 □ How many critical squares attend a typical passed pawn?

Normally three, which usually can be found two ranks ahead of the pawn. One critical square is on the same file as the pawn, and the other two are on the adjacent right and left files.

The only atypical passed pawn is the rook-pawn, which has only two critical squares.

385 □ Are a passed pawn's critical squares always the same, or do they shift?

The critical squares are not permanent (except for the rook-pawn), but change with the pawn's advance. If White has a passed pawn on e2, its critical squares are d4, e4, and f4. If this e2-pawn is the only pawn on the board, White can force a win by occupying any of these three squares (d4, e4, f4) with the king.

If the pawn moves to e3, the critical squares shift to d5, e5, and f5. If it moves to e4, the critical squares in turn become d6, e6, and f6 (which is where they stay if the pawn advances to e5, for pawns on the fourth and fifth ranks have the same critical squares).

The case of advancing to e6 is different, however, for the pawn shouldn't move there unless doing so confers the opposition, without giving check.

386 □ What formula determines the critical squares of rook-pawns?

Rook-pawns are a special case in that they have only two critical squares—knight-seven and knight-eight on the file adjacent to the pawn. Whether a rook-pawn is on a2, a3, a4, or a5, the critical squares are the same, b7 and b8. The attacker has only one concern. If the attacking king heads for b7 immediately, the enemy king can attempt to assail the pawn from the rear. This is usually telegraphed, though, and can be throttled.

387 □ Can both sides have critical squares in the same position?

Certainly every pawn, under the right circumstances, has the potential for a set of critical squares. A simple example is two opposing pawns blocking each other. Whichever side can occupy its pawn's critical squares first can force the win of the enemy pawn. (Critical squares for blocked opposing pawns, also known as fixed pawns, are different from those of ordinary passed pawns.) In some cases, however, even after the pawn is lost, the defender may still be able to draw by seizing the opposition.

OPPOSITIONS ATTRACT

388 □ What is the opposition?

The opposition is the relationship between the two kings when they stand head to head, fighting for the critical squares.

The kings "stand in opposition" when they: (1) occupy the same rank, file, or diagonal; (2) are on squares of the same color; and (3) are separated from each other by an odd number of squares (one, three, or five) along a straight line. The second and third criteria are inextricably linked.

389 □ Who has the advantage when the kings stand in opposition?

The one who stands and waits; that is, whichever king doesn't have to move. The player whose turn it is must make a declaration of intentions, and the other can then take advantage of it. The player not on the move "has the opposition," which is the same thing as saying "has the advantage."

If the attacker's king has the opposition, it can eventually force the occupation of critical squares, insuring a successful promotional pawn advance, with recourse to a turning maneuver at the key moment.

When the defender has the opposition, on the other hand, the attacker can be prevented from achieving these ends: no turning maneuver, no clearing of the way, no new queen.

390 □ Can the kings ever stand in opposition if they don't occupy the same rank, file, or diagonal?

If they don't occupy the same line, the kings might still stand in opposition if they occupy squares of the same color and if their relationship can be viewed in terms of a particular kind of rectangle.

Consider the smallest possible rectangle of squares containing the two kings. If the long and short sides of this rectangle are odd in number, then the kings stand in rectangular opposition (also called oblique opposition). Whoever doesn't move has the opposition, or the advantage. But this type of opposition is seldom tactically important, even in the fantasies of chess literature.

391 □ What is the distant opposition?

This is any opposition in which the kings stand on the same rank, file, or diagonal and are separated by either three or five squares (instead of one square). As with all oppositions, the kings must also occupy squares of the same color.

392 □ Which king is stronger when the two don't already stand in opposition?

The advantage generally passes to the king having the move. It can usually exploit the tempo to gain at least a temporary edge, moving into position to "take the opposition" to get the advantage. For the attacker, seizing the opposition usually wins; for the defender, it usually draws.

393 □ What are corresponding squares?

Corresponding squares are oppositional squares of mutual *zugzwang*, in which the oppositional field has been distorted by fixed and blocked pawns. This means the oppositional pattern is irregular, incapable of being determined by the usual methods. (For example, it usually doesn't matter whether the kings occupy same color squares or are separated by an odd number of squares along the same row.)

Corresponding squares are also known as associated squares, companion squares, conjugate squares, coordinate squares, corresponding oppositional squares, irregular oppositional squares, related squares, and sister squares. No wonder they're confusing.

Among the most difficult of endgame concepts, corresponding oppositional squares usually come in pairs, one for White and one for Black, and there may be a number of such pairs. They have relevance mainly in pure pawn endings, when the kings are the only pieces on the board, with the fight to exploit them sometimes extending across the entire board.

In corresponding square situations, each player wants the other to be the first to declare intentions and commit to a plan, idea, movement, maneuver, or sequence. Neither player's king should be moved to a corresponding square before its counterpart, for that would abandon the irregular opposition.

Thus, if a square the white king has access to corresponds to a square the black king has access to, White wants Black's king to go to its corresponding square before White's king goes to its corresponding square, and vice versa. Corresponding squares are booby traps. Step on them first and your world blows up (either you lose or fail to win a winning game).

MINOR PIECES, MAJOR PLAYERS

394 □ In king-and-rook-pawn vs. king situations, how helpful is the addition of a minor piece to the superior side?

Usually the addition of a minor piece helps achieve a win. The extra piece may be able to help stop the enemy king from occupying the corner square in front of the pawn. Or if the enemy king has already reached the corner, the piece may be able to attack the king and drive it out. The fly in the ointment is a "wrong-color bishop."

395 □ In the ending king, bishop, and rook-pawn vs. king, what's a wrong-color bishop?

A wrong-color bishop can't guard the promotion square, which is a different color from those the bishop travels on. The bishop is unable to check the cornered enemy king and the contest concludes in stalemate or draw by agreement.

Sometimes a draw results when a defender sacrifices or swaps down to stick the opponent with the wrong bishop. Sometimes it happens much earlier for unrelated reasons, before a serious endgame position arises.

396 □ Are there other cases where an extra minor piece can't insure the rook-pawn's promotion?

Another instance occurs when the knight is bolted down to protecting the pawn on rook-seven because the friendly king is away from the immediate area and can't help. If the defending king occupies the promotion square or can occupy it on the move, the superior side's king won't be able to move into position to protect the pawn (to free the knight from its defensive chore) without giving stalemate. This can be avoided if the pawn can defer moving to the seventh rank until its own king gets close enough to lend a hand. Then the win becomes a matter of repositioning the knight.

397 □ Do minor pieces sometimes have trouble defending against advanced rook-pawns?

Minor pieces lose the ability to operate on the other side of the pawn. The bishop, for example, can guard the queening square from only one diagonal. Often the attacker can drive the bishop off that diagonal, or intercept and block the diagonal so that the bishop no longer guards the queening square.

Knights, too, have problems against rook-pawns. In the center the knight attacks eight squares, but along the edge it attacks only four. When facing a rook-pawn, the knight cannot shift to the other side of the pawn to seek alternate defensive posts. The attacker may be able to prevent its approach to the queening area. And even if the knight reaches the queening square, it could still be trapped and won, for from the corner it has access to only two squares, both of which may be controlled or seized by the attacker.

398 □ Do knight-pawns also pose problems for minor pieces?

They can. For bishops, the problem is the length of the diagonals leading to the queening square. If the shortest defensive diagonal is too short (only two squares in length, for example), the attacker can often win by forcing the bishop to relinquish control of the promotion square.

Knights against knight-pawns can be bogged down as well. The chief difficulty is that sometimes the knight can't shift to the other side of the pawn, so it can be as impotent as it is against a rook-pawn.

399 □ Can a major piece without the immediate support of its own king stop a pawn from queening?

The queen can usually cope with a far-advanced pawn by forcing the enemy king in front of the pawn. Using either meaningful checks or pins, the pawn's advance can probably be prevented for at least one move. With that free move the attacker tries to bring the king closer, so the king and queen can eventually work together to win the pawn or set up checkmate. The process is then repeated, checks and pins, until the defending king is again forced in front of the pawn. The free move that results can be used to bring the attacking king yet another square closer. Eventually, the attacking king will be close enough to join forces with the queen, and the game soon ends.

The rook doesn't fare as well as the queen against a far-advanced pawn, and must often be sacrificed to prevent the pawn's queening. At that point, the position is drawn, stripped to bare essentials.

400 □ Can a king and a pawn draw against a king and a queen?

The queen often wins even against a pawn poised on its seventh rank, about to promote. There are two exceptions: rook-pawns and bishop-pawns. With either of these two pawns as allies, the defending king might be able to set up a stalemate by a timely movement to the corner.

This defense falters, however, when the attacking king is close enough to lend a hand. Then stalemate can be averted and the pawn is won or checkmate forced. Sometimes the mate occurs even after the pawn promotes, so that, in the final position, the material is equal, with both sides owning a queen. But the new queen is out of position to stop the checkmate.

401 □ Can a king and a pawn ever beat a king and a rook or a king and a queen?

Theoretically, they can. It's possible to construct a position in which, even with the move, the enemy rook can't stop the pawn from queening. In other instances, the pawn can promote to a queen, giving check. After the defending king gets out of check, the new queen repositions to deliver a winning fork or skewer or even checkmate. But such situations are mainly theoretical, rarely occuring in practice.

402 □ King, bishop, and pawn vs. king and minor piece: how should the inferior side defend?

Place the defending king in the pawn's path, on a square where it can't be checked. This blockades the pawn, allowing the defending minor piece to become active.

Sacrifice the piece for the pawn, of course, if the opportunity arises.

When your king can't get in front of the pawn, try to maneuver your king behind the pawn, attacking it from the rear. This may not draw, but it should provide the fiercest resistance, decreasing the enemy's winning chances and keeping you involved in the contest. Fight on.

403 □ Why do endings with bishops of opposite colors usually lead to a draw?

If one player is up a pawn, or even several pawns, the defending bishop and king can often establish an effective blockade. With bishops of opposite colors, though, the attacking bishop can't break the blockade, for it guards squares of only one color, the wrong one at that, and the game will probably peter out to a draw.

Suppose White has a king, a dark-square bishop, and two connected pawns placed diagonally on dark squares and on adjacent files. Black's king is on a light square blocking one of the pawns, while the black bishop, also on a light square, impedes the adjacent pawn. White's dark-square bishop can never lift this blockade because it can't guard light squares. Since Black can guard the light squares with two pieces and never has to relinquish them, White's pawns can't safely advance (they would be captured for nothing). The game is then a practical draw, since the superior side is unable to exploit its advantage and make progress.

A ROOK TO END IT ALL

404 □ What are the main weapons of a rook in the endgame?

A rook is a formidable piece, especially in attack. It's particularly lethal because it can: (1) manufacture a sudden mate; (2) attack or threaten from far away, with little chance of being counterattacked itself; (3) cordon or cut off entire sectors by occupying a rank or file, especially preventing the enemy king from crossing such barriers and participating in the fray.

405 □ What is the most important principle of rook endings?

There are so many principles for rook endings it's easy to get confused. If there's an overriding guideline, however, it's to keep your rook active and flexible. Don't tie your rook to defense. It needs to be able to attack from a distance, from the flank and from behind its target. Rooks love open files, and do very well on the seventh rank. They don't like defensive chores in front of their own pawns, though there are times when even this works.

406 □ What does the maxim "rooks belong behind passed pawns" mean?

This phrase refers to the optimal placement for a rook vis-à-vis a passed pawn. Whether attacking or defending, rooks occupying the same file as the pawn generally do better when positioned behind the pawn, where the rook's file mobility increases as the pawn advances. In many cases, to counter your rook's attack or support on the file, your opponent will station a rook on the same file in front of the pawn, so its file mobility *decreases* with the pawn's movement.

407 □ What is "building a bridge"?

This technique, named by Nimzovich, applies mainly to rook-and-pawn endings. The idea is to create a shelter for your king from enemy rook checks by interposing your own rook, protected by your king. This measure stops the checks and insures the promotion of a dangerous pawn, usually already on the seventh rank. The concept is often explained by illustrating the "Lucena position," an example first published in 1634 by Salvio. Lucena died in the 16th century, having had nothing to do with the position named after him.

408 □ What's the difference between an active rook defense and a passive one?

A rook defends actively if it attempts to attack from the rear or from the flank. To achieve such activity, it's often worthwhile to sacrifice a pawn or two. On the one hand, a rook defends passively when it's tied to protecting a pawn and is unable to move without abandoning the pawn. But a rook also defends passively when it merely occupies its home rank, warding off checkmate or other unpleasant enemy rook invasions. An active rook stirs up counterplay; a passive one just sits, guards, and waits.

409 □ **H**ow far away from its target does a rook have to be before it becomes effective?

A rook is a long-range piece, increasing in strength the farther it gets from its victim, because then it can attack with less chance of being counterattacked. It operates at full strength when there are at least three squares between itself and its object of attack. When it's this far away from the enemy passed pawn, we say the rook has the "checking distance." A king, checked by such a distant rook, can't stop the attacks by approaching the rook without endangering its own pawn. When the rook doesn't have the checking distance, if it's not far enough away, the enemy king may indeed be able to approach the rook and end the checks without making concessions.

410 □ **W**hat should I do if the enemy rook that was cutting off my king's participation has abandoned the cut-off?

Do what you were prevented from doing earlier: move the king to the sector or square the enemy rook previously stopped your king from reaching. Very often the king's sudden entrance or reemergence on the scene, guarding key squares or supporting certain ambitions, saves the day. Better yet, save the day, seize the rook.

411 □ **W**hat is Philidor's draw?

Philidor's draw is a way of setting up a positional draw in rook-and-pawn endings. The defending rook occupies its own third rank, cutting off the advance of the enemy passed pawn and king. For the attacking king to advance, the pawn must move first, creating a shield for the king and breaking the rook's control of the rank. But then the defending rook shifts to its last (eighth) rank, preparing to check the enemy king from behind. This position is then drawable, since there is no place for the attacking king to escape from the rook checks.

If the pawn doesn't advance, remaining on the fifth rank instead, the king could escape rearward rook checks by moving to the sixth rank, hiding in front of the pawn. But, alas, you can't have everything.

412 □ **W**hat's the most important principle of queen endings?

In an endgame where a queen, king, and pawns face a queen, king, and pawns, you can get a lot of mileage out of your own queen by placing it in the center, if this can be done safely and satisfactorily. By occupying the center, your queen prevents the opposing queen from doing so, denying it increased scope and possibilities, diminishing its chances to check and threaten.

413 □ What happens when, with no pawns on the board, a king and a rook face a king and a minor piece?

This slight material disparity usually leads to a draw. When the minor piece is a knight, the defender must be careful to keep king and knight together to guard the knight. If the two are separated so that the knight needs two or more moves to get back to the king's protection, and it's also the attacker's turn, the knight is almost always lost by force. Separation of a king and bishop, however, is usually no problem, for the long-range bishop can get back in one move, no matter how far away it is.

As a defender, it's best to keep your king off the edge, out of the corners, and in the center. The edge allows the opponent to play for mate, often combined with double attack (an additional threat to capture the piece).

The corner can be a death trap. King and knight tangled in the corner is the worst. If you don't lose in this situation, somebody up there likes you. With a king and a bishop, there are two losing corners and two safe ones. To draw, you'd better find out quickly which is which.

414 □ Which corners afford the safest retreat for the king and bishop in the endgame king-and-rook vs. king-and-bishop?

The safest corners are those opposite in color from the squares on which the bishop travels. If you have a light-square bishop and you are driven back, head toward the dark squares a1 or h8. If you have a dark-square bishop, head for the light squares a8 or h1.

415 □ How are king-and-rook vs. king-and-bishop endgames actually won?

After driving the inferior king to the edge, the attacker tries to threaten checkmate and the bishop simultaneously. If the bishop is used as a shield to block checks along the edge, the rook pins the bishop. The king is then constrained to move away from the bishop, and the rook captures the bishop on the next turn. If you, the attacker, need to gain a tempo after the bishop is pinned, merely shift the rook a square or two along the same row as the pin, making sure not to fall off the edge.

416 □ Why doesn't the technique of pinning the bishop to the king work when the king retreats to a safe corner?

If the king and bishop occupy squares near a safe corner, it doesn't work because the rook can't temporize along the edge to win the bishop: the king defending the bishop has no available square for occupation and stalemate results. Should the king withdraw toward the wrong corner, however, mate rears by forcing the bishop into a pin and, if needed, making a tempo move with the rook.

417 □ How does a game end when a king, a rook, and a minor piece oppose a king and a rook, and there are no pawns on the board?

This scenario normally settles down to a theoretical draw. When the minor piece is a knight, practice and theory marry. Hardly ever does the side with the knight win, and a draw usually results.

A bishop is a special goody, however. With this minor piece the attacker wins more often than not. This doesn't mean endgame theory is undependable. But chess is much more than theory. Practical difficulties can cost the defender a theoretically tenable position.

418 □ Why is it so difficult for the defender to draw with king, rook, and bishop against king and rook, even though the ending is a theoretical draw?

The problems begin once the defending king has been driven to the edge of the board, which is what usually happens. Trapped along the edge, the king is subject to long-term mating threats. They shouldn't be fatal, but the complexity of working through the maze of possibilities invites costly errors. The defender may need to keep alert for stretches of twenty or thirty moves, at a time when momentary lapses are difficult to avoid.

419 □ Why would a player with an advantage in an endgame repeat the position on purpose, without making any tangible headway?

The inferior side in an endgame doesn't mind repetitions, hoping to save the game by a threefold repetition. But the superior side can avoid this by never allowing the position to be repeated more than twice. Twice is okay when you are trying to: (1) learn something or get a better feel for a position; (2) see if the opponent will err the second time around; (3) gain time on the clock, to make it easier to reach the time control without forfeiting; or (4) recreate a favorable position not capitalized on the first time it occurred.

One endgame principle warns not to rush into anything not clearly desirable, which is why many teachers say: "don't hurry." One aspect of this approach, is to be willing to repeat the position just to see what happens the second time, assuming such an action doesn't risk dissipating your advantage, however small.

420 □ Which are the most important endgames to study?

Fifty percent of all endgames include rooks and a hundred percent include kings! Queen endings and minor-piece endings happen somewhat less often because these pieces are more easily exchanged. So, based on frequency of occurrence, it seems sensible to emphasize endings with just pawns, as well as those with rooks and pawns. But it can't hurt to make endgame analysis a lifetime project. Try it for a while and see what happens.

10

SITUATIONAL PSYCHOLOGY

BLUNDERING BLITHELY ALONG

421 □ **D**oes a blunder automatically lose?

A blunder may actually only be a stumble. Sure, blundering can lead to checkmate or loss of your queen, but sometimes it merely throws away your advantage. Anyway, there's no guarantee your opponent will capitalize on an error. In most games, the winner makes at least several mistakes and gets away with them. I've seen countless games, some between world class players, in which one side blundered into mate and the other missed it. The chess world is populated by survivors.

Blunders, however, often matter. A game's outcome tends to be determined by common mistakes and oversights, and the better player usually commits fewer errors. If you never err, you never lose. But you can blunder without losing, and it's not uncommon to make several mistakes and still avert defeat. You can blunder and your opponent falters in turn, hence the maxim: "the winner is the one who makes the next to last mistake."

422 □ What should I do if I blunder?

Don't panic. If you've erred out of carelessness, you wouldn't want to continue in that vein, leading to a worse mistake and sudden loss. Besides, your opponent may not realize your blunder. Better not let the enemy know by becoming upset. Don't give off any disaster signals.

Should your opponent spot your error and exploit it, don't be fazed. Take a break before playing your next move. Regain your composure and you may be able to resist, or even induce your opponent into blundering in turn. It may save a losing game.

423 □ What kinds of blunders occur most often?

The most common blunders are: (1) overlooking the enemy threat; (2) moving a unit where it can be captured for nothing; (3) unguarding a unit; and (4) failing to recapture.

424 □ How can I reduce blunders in my own play?

Be more careful. Don't play automatically. Really try to understand your opponent's moves before responding to them. Don't make the mistake of pursuing your own plans in a vacuum, without regard to your opponent's play. To help yourself in this quest, ask yourself questions about your opponent's apparent plans, such as: "What's the reason for that?" Whatever and however, slow down and use your time prudently.

425 □ Are there practical exercises to reduce blunders?

Without a doubt, you can reduce blundering by developing certain habits of mind. There are many things you can try. For instance, whenever you see a chess game or position in a book, simply run through a set of basic calculations. If you practice this analysis daily, it will become a matter-of-fact procedure that will carry over to your own play and reduce your tendency to make obvious mistakes, such as leaving pieces unprotected or not defending against mate threats.

Determine, for both sides: (1) the material situation (who's ahead); (2) immediate threats to material or the king, and how these threats can be answered (for example, find out if attacked units are sufficiently guarded); and (3) potential targets and weak points for future attacks (both for you and to you), and how these threats can be developed or averted.

426 □ How do I avoid getting mated on the back rank?

You can get mated along the back rank (your own first rank) by an enemy rook or queen, especially when your king is castled kingside and none of your major pieces occupy your first rank. You can prevent this mate by being careful, but if you're afraid your attention might wander, you can protect yourself for the future by making *luft*. You do this by moving a pawn in front of your king, clearing an escape hatch for the king and enabling it to flee the first rank if checked.

427 □ Which is the best kingside pawn to use in making *luft*?

In general, the best pawn to move to make *luft* is the h-pawn because its advance creates fewer weaknesses than result from moving the g-pawn or the f-pawn. But even if you make *luft* your opponent may be able to guard the escape hatch, retaining the possibility of a back-rank mate. You can counter this by playing with your eyes open, which may even give you the advantage.

428 □ Should I think one way on my move and another way on my opponent's move?

Be definite when it's your turn, addressing your opponent's last move while maximizing your own pressure. You have to put it all together and find the best move.

On your opponent's turn, however, you are less beset with immediate pressures. You can let your mind wander, scavenging for information on future attacks and plans and uncovering weak points and targets. Think specifically on your turn, and generally on your opponent's.

429 □ After calculating a long variation, is there something I can do as a final safeguard to avoid error?

You can't avoid error, but you can reduce its likelihood. You can do this by making sure that, at the end of your calculations, your opponent doesn't have a capture or especially a check to overturn the whole applecart.

We often look for and note these enemy possibilities before beginning our calculations. But once we get involved in a deep line of analysis, it's easy to forget our earlier conclusions. The way we can bring them back into focus is by asking: "Can my opponent interfere with this line of analysis by a check or a capture"? This won't insure your safety, but it won't hurt either.

MIRROR, MIRROR

430 □ What should I calculate first, a two-move threat to win the queen or a three-move threat to checkmate?

Either one can be a valid starting point. It makes sense to begin with the simplest two-move calculation, which usually requires the fewest moves to see ahead. Sometimes a three-move threat is simpler to calculate because the opponent has fewer or more limited responses.

Generally, if two or more attacking ideas occur to you simultaneously, take the most direct and simplest. After you're certain of the consequences of the more obvious sequence, consider the more complicated possibilities. Then you can decide which line of attack is really best.

If the more complex lines prove to be too difficult to determine accurately, at least you know you can fall back on the simpler, clearer variation you've already calculated.

431 □ How sensible is it to subject a position to a preliminary evaluation before doing a thorough one?

Most of the time it's a good idea because it allows you to arrange candidate moves in terms of worth. You can begin analyzing the more likely possibilities first. If you start by considering the first plausible idea that surfaces, you can wind up wasting time on an inferior move you'd better not play.

A preliminary analysis, however superficial, tends to save time by paring bad ideas down to create a core list of reasonable ones. From that group of candidate moves, eliminate some and rate what remains according to priority and predictability.

Use your head. Think, and think some more.

432 □ **W**hen analyzing a sequence of moves in my head, if I notice that on the third move of the sequence my opponent has two possible replies, how should I proceed?

You can only analyze one move at a time, so in your head you have to pick one of the two moves for your opponent, mentally play it on the board, and continue analyzing from that situation. Since you probably won't know which of the two enemy moves is the one to consider first, just pick according to your intuition. Take heed, however. After considering the first move, make sure you consider the second one. The only time you don't also analyze the second move is if you determine that the first move is so desirable for your opponent (it mates or forces an easily won game) that there's no need to look further. Keep it simple. Don't get tied up in analytic knots. Make a good decision and play it.

433 □ **H**ow many moves ahead should I calculate?

The purpose of looking ahead is to determine the future, to avert badness and to insure goodness. When you consider any series of moves, mentally you must be able to evaluate the position at the end of your analysis. This can be done if the position itself is relatively quiet, with no immediate threats for either side. You might have to look ahead just a few moves to imagine such a position, or maybe you'll need to "see" somewhat further than that.

If there's no light at the end of the tunnel, or if the resulting position is too unstable, don't bother looking further. Just start considering a simpler line that's easier to comprehend and takes fewer moves to visualize and understand.

A newcomer shouldn't attempt to look too far ahead. Be practical. Try to consider your opponent's likely responses and respond accordingly.

434 □ **W**hat's the meaning of counting in chess?

Counting has several different meanings. The most common is counting and comparing the forces, to determine if either side has a material advantage. If the play is focused on a particular square, we may also count defenders and attackers and compare them, to see who has control over the square. And counting is also a reference. As in king-and-pawn endings, you might count the number of moves it takes to make a new queen, thus determining which side queens first.

435 □ How do I know if I control a square?

Count the number of units you have attacking it and subtract the number of units your opponent uses to defend it. If the involved forces are of the same quality (pawn vs. pawn, knight vs. knight, rook vs. rook, queen vs. queen), you have the advantage if your attackers outnumber your opponent's defenders. If attackers equal defenders, however, defenders are in control.

If the quality of attacking and defending units is not the same, pawn control tends to decide and could compensate for what might otherwise be a deficiency. Generally, less valuable units (pawns and minor pieces) are better for controlling squares because they are more expendable than rooks and queens.

MOVEMENT IMPROVEMENT

436 □ What kinds of problems do inexperienced players have?

There are many pitfalls for the newcomer and relative beginner. As a group, they may complicate their chess in some or all of the following ways: (1) by making gross mistakes, such as leaving their own threatened units unprotected or failing to capture unprotected enemy units; (2) by not knowing the relative values of the pieces, or by not taking these values into account when exchanging; (3) by playing too passively, permitting their opponent virtual freedom of action; (4) by having no understanding of positional strengths and weaknesses; (5) by being unable to analyze and calculate forced sequences; (6) by playing planlessly and by not thinking strategically; and (7) generally by playing moves without purpose.

The aimless tendencies of games contested between some amateurs can be quite amusing. As a chess teacher, I try to have compassion for these unschooled warriors. But it's often amusing to watch an entire game in which winning advantages shift back and forth, from White to Black, until someone wins by accident.

437 □ What special qualities make for success in chess?

Success in chess is a complex matter. There is no definitive answer, although many say, perhaps simplistically, that the most valuable quality for a successful chessplayer is a flair for spatial relations. Other theories include a good memory, a sense for logical sequence, a talent for analogies and pattern recognition, the killer instinct, and good concentration. Learning at an early age also helps.

Alexander Alekhine (1892–1946), one of the foremost world chess champions, had another idea. He felt that one must be level-headed about one's own strengths and weaknesses. Equally necessary was to be objective in understanding an opponent's pluses and minuses. Moreover, one had to be more concerned with long-term goals rather than immediate gains, both in individual games and in the development of one's career. In this latter sense, Alekhine equated chess with art and science.

438 □ What is the "quantum theory" of chess improvement?

Essentially, the quantum theory asserts that people seem to make periodic and sudden jumps in chess improvement, rather than continuous and fluid ones.

Chess education offers peaks and plateaus, and learning the game goes something like this: Let's say to climb to the next level of skill you must learn a thousand things. If you've learned 999 of those things, obviously you should be a much better player than when you knew nothing, but you may not necessarily show significant improvement yet. You still may not be able to implement certain acquired skills, so your overall play appears relatively the same.

But add that last piece of knowledge (the thousandth thing!) and suddenly, seemingly inexplicably, you jump to the next skill level. You've finally put it all together, and your ability has taken a quantum leap.

439 □ What is the first thing I need to do in order to improve at chess?

Learn to be objective. Don't be emotional about moves. When considering a position during a game, try to determine what's actually happening on the board. And when the contest is over, try to comprehend what really happened, analyzing the game to see how you could have played better (better is almost always possible).

There's a tendency to excuse one's shortcomings and defeats. Emanuel Lasker (1868–1941), world champion for twenty-seven years, from 1894 to 1921, explained such rationalizations: "I never beat a well man." Sound familiar?

440 □ How many hours a day should I study chess?

As many as you can, preferably no less than ten—if you want to be Bobby Fischer or Garry Kasparov. If you are a newcomer and would simply like to get a little better, a couple of hours a week is fine. Serious players between these two extremes should put in about six hours a week, divided into three sessions. But it's up to you. Just how much are you willing to sacrifice for the world's greatest game?

441 □ How can I improve my defense?

Improving defensive play is one of the hardest things to do in chess. If you find books on the subject, such as Andrew Soltis's excellent work, *The Art of Defense in Chess*, get them and study them. You might also turn to the games of the great defensive players. Even though their overall styles are different, the games of Lasker, Botvinnik, Petrosian, Korchnoi, and Karpov illustrate how to hold onto material, and when to give it back.

You would also do well to develop a particular habit of mind. Instead of analyzing a position to find what's the best move for you, turn the picture around. Pretend it's your opponent's move and try to imagine potential attacks against you. This will quickly help you focus on your weak points and vulnerabilities, and puts a whole new slant on things most players never consider. This new perspective won't make you a defensive genius, but you'll probably get mated a lot less and lose fewer pawns and pieces. That's good chess, no matter what kind of player you are.

442 □ Should I play the board or the opponent?

No matter what else you do, always play the board. It's right in front of you and can't lie. It's the universe where you, the chessplayer, live and die. But if you know your opponents and understand their styles, or if somehow during play they reveal their intentions, or if you've seen their past games in the opening at hand, or if you can read their faces or bodies, or if a reliable palm reader gives you inside information, use it. It's life, it's war, it's chess, and everything matters.

443 □ What's more important: study or play?

Authorities are divided on this question.

Some say study has greater value, arguing that chess is mainly a mental activity, and is best learned through literature and home analysis. Why take an hour to play a game when you can read through several annotated games in the same time?

Others counter that chess is still a game, and to be understood and appreciated in context, must be experienced under game conditions. If you followed tennis but never played, are you likely to be a good tennis player?

Any ratio of play and study could work for a given individual. However, if you want to become a strong player, you'll probably develop faster with a healthy diet of both theory and practice—as much as you can get of each.

RECORD DISTRACTION

444 □ How can keeping score help me reduce blunders?

Writing down your moves before playing them is an old chess trick to reduce the chances for error. It works this way. After you've decided on your move, write it on the scoresheet and take a moment to consider it one more time. You are providing yourself an opportunity to make one last careful check of enemy threats, to see if you've missed something obvious. In fact, the actual writing of the move may trigger unconscious thoughts, stopping you from playing an error or doing something you may come to regret.

445 □ Doesn't writing my move before playing it give my opponents advance knowledge of my plan and provide them with extra time to analyze?

It telegraphs your intentions, but don't worry about it. If it's a good move, your opponent will be the one to worry. And if the move is atrocious, your foe's body movement or facial expression may be a red flag, warning you that you're about to make a fatal mistake. If you discern something wrong, simply erase the move and start thinking again. There's no penalty (it's perfectly legitimate) and you avoid a pitfall.

446 □ Is there a best move in every situation?

If you have but one single legal move, that's your best. If a move forces checkmate, or is the only one to gain a definite advantage, it too must be the best. But in many situations it's impossible to decide on the best move, so we settle for a good one and try to support it with a logical plan.

Someday computers may be able to provide the best move in all cases. But until then the question of the best move cannot be satisfactorily answered. We don't even know if there's a best first move to start the game. Though according to Bobby Fischer, beginning a game as White by advancing the e-pawn two squares is "best by test." He must mean *his* test.

447 □ Why do some chess teachers de-emphasize the importance of pawn weaknesses?

Teachers sometimes play down pawn weaknesses with certain beginning students who may become so concerned with doubled and isolated pawns that more relevant factors are neglected. Students should be encouraged to avoid weakening pawn moves, but not to the extent of abandoning material or allowing themselves to be checkmated.

Let's get our priorities straight. Most games between amateurs are decided by direct threats and attacks, not by subtle maneuvering against weak squares. I've often seen students fail to recapture in front of their castled positions because they dreaded the doubled pawns and the slight exposure of their kings that would result. Instead, by not taking back, they opted for a definite loss of material and almost certain defeat.

448 □ Can a computer help in a lesson?

A computer can help in a number of ways. My favorite is for the student and teacher to play as a team against the computer, analyzing the game in progress. For this purpose, it doesn't matter if the "student" is an individual, several persons in a semi-private lesson, or an entire class. But it may be of greatest value to a single student.

Typically, a teacher questions a student's thinking processes sometime after a game's completion. At that point, the student probably has forgotten the reasons for certain moves. However, because the teacher can ask probing questions right on the spot, the immediacy of a computer game can reveal vexing problems that might not otherwise come out.

The ongoing discussion not only helps the teacher but also shows the student how to handle specific problems without changing the computer's response. In discussing a game in progress between two actual people, the defender learns of the attacker's plans and can try to counteract them. The aims are thereby thwarted. A computer plays on blindly, however, falling right into traps set by the student-teacher team. The lesson works and it's swell recreation.

449 □ **W**ouldn't it be an equally effective lesson to record a game and examine it at a later time with my teacher, instead of using a computer?

Reviewing a previously recorded game with a teacher may have great value. But it lacks immediacy and is therefore less efficacious than discussing a game in progress. No matter how carefully you play over a recorded game, fine points tend to be forgotten and half-conscious plans and misconceptions are never brought up at all. The best learning occurs on the spot, as it actually happens.

A LESSON FROM THE MASTER

450 □ **S**hould my chess lessons be structured?

An overwhelming number of people think so, but this is a popular misconception. The most important thing to learn is how to analyze chess positions. You need an approach, rather than an encyclopedia of information.

Many good chess teachers simply review the games their students play, asking questions and making suggestions, and engaging their students in give-and-take. Active exchanges of this kind, even when the positions analyzed are selected at random, have far more vitality and effect than the cold type of the best chess books. So get your structure, if you think you need it. But I prefer learning how to think.

451 □ **I**s it better to analyze by yourself or with others?

Both ways can be good. Before you start to do either one, however, you must learn how to analyze. This too you can do by yourself or with others, preferably with a teacher or a sympathetic master.

Once you've learned how to analyze you'll find that when you do it by yourself your concentration is stronger and you see more. But it's tough to be level-headed, and the presence of another analyst imposes objectivity, countering the natural bias that comes from sitting on one side of the board. The chief drawback is that your co-analyst could as easily lead you down the wrong path with overly persuasive reasoning (speaking faster or louder). Know anyone like that?

452 □ Is it better to study all of the openings or just a few?

For a newcomer, it makes sense to study just a few openings and to learn them well. As you get more practiced in a few good beginnings, you'll learn certain principles that apply across the board. Then you can familiarize yourself with other openings, and as you gradually and naturally expand your repertoire, you can better decide which openings to focus on more seriously—the ones you really like.

453 □ What's the best way to start studying a particular opening?

There's no consensus on this question, but I say start by playing through complete games, all in the opening of your choice. Select games with plenty of verbal and analytic notes, especially if at least one of the players is strong.

Take an historical approach. Try to learn the original reasons for the openings and their moves (when they were first tried in games played years ago), and why we play them differently now. Play through fifty or a hundred games this way, carefully examining every note. You can find the games in books, magazines, newspapers, wherever.

While doing this, you may accumulate questions about the opening moves. Write them down in a book so you can review them or show them to a teacher. Track down one or more opening manuals to see what moves they recommend in the variations you're researching. This way, you won't just be memorizing moves, but understanding ideas in context.

454 □ When studying an annotated game, would it help if I reviewed the diagrams before playing through the moves?

Familiarity with the diagrams certainly adds to awareness of what's happening. Usually, diagrams are given either just before or just after critical positions. From the diagrammed position, it may be possible to pinpoint a winning move, a key defense, a surprise shot, some resource furthering a plan, or any move the annotator deemed worthy.

Reviewing the diagrams before the game outlines the terrain. When you then play over the game, you're better able to follow the genesis and evolution of the key themes: the diagrams are signposts that tell you what to expect.

455 □ **W**hich are the best kinds of games for an amateur to play over: games between other amateurs or games between grandmasters?

Neither type is good for the amateur. Games between grandmasters are so removed from the amateur's experience that they have limited practical value, and often seem to make no sense. The amateur's typical errors are not seen in these games, and there really isn't a common ground for understanding.

Reviewing games between two amateurs is also pointless. It's true that amateurish errors are made, but they're not often punished, and that attenuates the instruction.

The ideal games to analyze are those between amateurs and grandmasters. The amateurs make the usual mistakes, and the grandmasters refute the bad play, which makes for powerful instruction. Suddenly the game offers meaning and logic and learners can grasp what to avoid in their own play and also how to exploit similarly weak play by their opponents. The problem is, it's not easy to find games between amateurs and grandmasters. Perhaps computers will soon be able to generate such material.

11

COMBAT
AND
COMPETITION

456 □ **D**oes playing speed chess with a clock help or hinder one's game?

Speed chess can be quite helpful. You spend your time learning to be aggressive. Most speed games (also called rapid transit) are won by the side that pushes and forces matters, since more thinking time is needed for proper defense. Speed play also develops your tactical and combinative skills. And you play many more games and experience more chess than usual.

Undeniably, though, it's superficial. It encourages direct attacks, and since you don't have the time to analyze them sufficiently, you could be stuck with a flawed plan. Speed chess is bad training for you when your opponent has more time to think and analyze. As a carryover from speed contests, you may play thin or unsound attacks, simply moving too quickly. Your opponent, on the other hand, isn't compelled to respond quickly, but can sit back and find the refutation to your overanxious moves.

Speed chess is enjoyable on its own terms. But never, never consider it during tournament play, unless, of course, it's a speed chess tournament!

457 □ What is blindfold chess?

In blindfold chess at least one of the participants plays "blindly," either by having his or her eyes covered or by sitting facing away from the board. Moves are conveyed in chess notation. In most cases, it's played by strong players to impress an audience.

If a player engages several games of blindfold chess at the same time, it's a blindfold simultaneous. The record for the most blindfold games conducted simultaneously is fifty-two, held by Janos Flesch of Hungary.

Among the great blindfold players was the American Harry Nelson Pillsbury (1872–1906). Supposedly, he could play twenty games of chess blindfolded simultaneously while also playing twenty simultaneous blindfold games of checkers and a hand of whist. In addition, before the start of the exhibition, he would memorize a list of forty long, obscure words given to him by the audience, reciting them at the beginning and at the end of the exhibition. And throughout the entire business he would carry on witty conversation.

458 □ When playing against a blindfolded player, is the best strategy to create confusion by playing peculiar moves?

If you want to lose quickly, playing bizarre moves is the way to do it. Rather than confuse the blindfolded player, it aids memory because it stamps the position indelibly.

For example, starting the game with a2-a4 or h2-h4 is unforgettable and stands out like a sore thumb. It's better to play fairly standard moves, with the possibility of nuances and subtle transpositions. Blindfolded players are then more likely to be lulled into "oversights." Because of their familiarity with the given position, they may even think they've already played a move they meant to but didn't.

459 □ What should my plan be if my opponent assumes a material handicap, such as starting the game without a queen-rook?

Your plan of action will of course depend on whether you have White or Black, how much of a handicap you receive, and the strength of your opponent. But regardless of this, since you already have a decisive advantage, you should try to simplify ruthlessly and avoid making moves that would complicate the winning process.

Generally, the more you trade, the less fight your opponent has. In particular, exchange the queens as soon as possible. And don't get overly materialistic, grabbing poisoned pawns and passively protecting irrelevant ones. That's like signing your own death warrant.

If you have an extra rook, you don't need more material to win. In fact, with the great advantage of an extra rook, you can afford to give back some of your material (such as a pawn or two), if it breaks your opponent's attack and busts the game. You'll still be ahead and life will be easier.

RATING THE RATINGS

460 □ What is an Elo rating?

An Elo rating is a number, usually four digits, that fairly accurately signifies relative playing ability. It is determined by results in rated tournament and match games, and subject to up-and-down changes based on subsequent results. If you win a rated game, you gain points; if you lose a game, you lose points; and if you draw, you gain points if your opponent was higher rated and you lose points if your opponent was lower rated. The method for calculating this number was introduced by Kenneth Harkness (1898–1972) and later developed and promoted by Arpad Elo (1903–   ), a Hungarian-born American mathematician.

A modified Elo rating system used in the U.S. assigns players to classes based on rating: the higher the number, the stronger the player. A B-player is rated between 1600 and 1799; an A-player 1800–1999; an expert 2000–2199; and a master 2200 and above. Most international grandmasters fall between 2500 and 2700. The highest-rated players of all time, according to the international list, are Garry Kasparov (2800 in 1990), and Bobby Fischer (2785 in 1972).

461 □ What is the rating of the average U.S. tournament player?

The rating system is geared for an average player of 1500, but in practice it gravitates toward 1400. Class D is 1200–1399, and Class C is 1400–1599, so the average rated player is a Class C player.

As far as unrated players go (casual players who do not compete in tournaments), the bulk exhibit a playing strength somewhere between 1000 to 1400. Though undoubtedly many rank lower, some unrated players may be the equivalent of chess masters in ability (around 2200).

462 □ What determines a strong player?

Although not everyone agrees, I consider strong players to begin around 1800, or class A.

I consider a player strong if, given most kinds of winning advantages, the player is capable of selecting a reasonable winning plan and implementing it correctly so that victory is usually achieved. Occasionally weaker players may also choose the right plans and execute them properly, but they'll succeed less often.

Generally, a higher rating indicates greater strength. But not all players with high ratings are truly strong. Whom they faced in tournaments, the ratings of their opponents, and even the circumstances under which they played must be considered. Did they beat up on beginners or did they defeat world class players? Such things are not necessarily reflected in a rating.

463 □ How can I get a rating?

You get a rating by playing tournament games sanctioned by the U.S. Chess Federation (USCF). It's very easy. First become a member of the USCF, which is the official governing body of U.S. chess. You can then play in a rated tournament.

Most tournaments are listed in *Chess Life,* the USCF's monthly magazine, which all members receive (junior players can get a scholastic publication instead). You can pick out a tournament, register, and then show up and play. You can even join the USCF at the tournament site, if you prefer. It's that simple.

464 □ How can I find out about chess events in the United States?

You can start by contacting the U.S. Chess Federation, which publishes lists of rated tournaments around the U.S. in its magazine *Chess Life. Chess Life* also presents news and other useful information on chess here and worldwide. Its address is: U.S. Chess Federation, 186 Route 9W, New Windsor, New York, 12550 (914-562-8350).

You can also look up chess clubs in your area. Just about every city has one, and often such organizations are affiliates of the USCF. The two most famous American chess clubs are the Manhattan and the Marshall, both in New York City. Their addresses are: Manhattan Chess Club, 353 W. 46th Street, New York, NY, 10036 (212-333-5888); and Marshall Chess Club, 23 West 10th Street, New York, NY, 10011 (212-477-3716).

Your local library can be a big help. In addition to providing literature and other references on the royal game, the library may be where the local chess club meets. You can also contact your local newspaper, especially if it has a chess column. And finally, if you're a student, see if there's a chess team or club in your school. You can join, take classes, or simply meet other people interested in the game.

There are plenty of opportunities out there for those with chess fever.

465 □ What does "touch move" really mean?

"Touch move" is a rule that requires you to move whatever unit you touch, unless you've first indicated your intention to adjust a unit. You must move or capture the first unit touched, regardless of which others are subsequently touched on the same turn. If a friendly unit is touched, you must move it. If an enemy unit is touched, you must capture it.

If you touch a friendly unit and then an enemy unit, you must try to capture the enemy unit with the friendly unit. If this is illegal, you may make any legal move with the friendly unit, without feeling obliged to capture anything. If there's no legal move with the touched friendly unit, you may make any legal move with any friendly unit.

If you touch an enemy unit first and then a friendly unit second, you must capture the enemy unit with the friendly unit. If this is illegal, you must capture the enemy unit with something else. If this is impossible, you may play any legal move.

466 □ How can I straighten out my pieces without being called for "touch move"?

Just before touching units you wish to fix, simply say "I adjust" or "adjust." Worldwide, the French *j'adoube* is used to mean the same thing. After declaring your intention, go ahead and straighten your forces. It should be the least of your worries.

467 □ When is a move completed?

If it's an ordinary move, such as the transfer of a unit from one square to another, it's completed when you release the unit. If it's a capture, it's completed when you've removed the captured unit from the board and, having placed the capturing unit on the square, removed your hand from it.

For castling, the move is completed when you have released the rook after it has crossed the king (or when you have released the king after it has crossed the rook, though you should try to move your king first). And on promotion, it's when the pawn has been removed from the board and you have released the new piece.

JOUSTING AT TOURNAMENTS

468 □ What is the procedure for adjourning a game in a tournament or match?

To adjourn a game, you call over the tournament director or referee, say that you want to seal a move, and ask for the envelope. Decide on your move, write it down on your score sheet, put it inside and seal the envelope, and, finally, stop your clock.

The referee will confirm that the position you've indicated on the outside of the envelope is correct (there may be a blank diagram or simply a place to record the pieces and pawns). It should be the position just before the sealed move.

The amount of time each player has used will be recorded on the outside of the envelope. Also given will be the names of the players, including who sealed and the number of the sealed move. The players will then agree on a playoff time, unless this has already been decided for them by the rules of the event.

469 □ What is the difference between a tournament and a match?

A tournament, whether Swiss, round-robin, or knock-out, must start with at least three players, and usually has many more than that.

The larger open tournaments may have as many as a thousand players. A match, on the other hand, has only two contestants who play a certain number of games with each other (usually at least two).

Sometimes the concepts blend, as in a knock-out match tournament, where more than two players face off in a series of elimination matches, as in tennis tournaments where those who advance must win two out of three sets or three out of five sets. There are also matches between teams, each having a certain number of players. If each team has four players, for example, the first boards of each team play one or more games against each other; second boards play against second boards; and so on. In the end, the results of each team's individual match-ups are added up to determine the winning team.

470 □ What is a Swiss tournament?

A Swiss tournament permits many people to participate, compared with a round-robin or knock-out tournament. A typical Swiss has four to six rounds. The underlying idea is that contestants mainly face players with like scores, exceptions being made only when necessary. Losers play losers and winners play winners (if possible).

In a round-robin tournament, everyone plays everyone. And in a knock-out (elimination) tournament, losers are out of the tournament; in a double elimination event, you must lose twice to be eliminated. But whether the tournament requires single or double elimination, the sole survivor is the winner.

471 □ In terms of scoring in a tournament or match, how many points each are a win, a loss, and a draw worth?

For every chess game, a total of one point is offered for White's and Black's efforts combined. If you win, you get a point and your opponent gets nothing. If you lose, you come away with nothing and your opponent is given a point. In the event of a draw, each player gets half a point.

472 □ If the game is drawn, do I have to replay it?

Drawn games are normally not replayed. Half a point is added to each player's score, just as a winning player receives one point and a losing player gets nothing.

In the last century and the early part of this one, certain tournament organizers experimented with different ways of treating draws, including replaying them or counting a draw as a quarter of a point. But these curiosities never caught on.

WIN, LOSE, DRAW

473 □ **H**ow can two players tie for first in a tournament, yet one is declared the overall winner?

It's not unusual for several players to tie for first in a tournament. Usually all of them are considered winners of the tournament and share the prize money. When two tie for first, they generally combine the first and second prizes and each gets half of the total. When three tie, they split first, second, and third. But there's probably only one first-place trophy, so there has to be a fair way to determine who should get it.

Because it's impractical in most cases to have playoffs to determine an absolute winner, a tie-breaking system is necessary. The various types of tie-breaking systems are usually based on the scores of the opponents each player faced. In theory, regardless of the precise method for interpreting the results, the winner should be the player whose opposition had the highest scores.

474 □ **H**ow do players agree to draw a game?

Draws by mutual agreement take place when one player simply offers a draw and the other accepts. In tournament and sanctioned match play, however, there's a further requirement. The draw offer must be made at the proper time, which is the moment when the player proposing the draw makes a move. The opponent can then respond verbally, taking as much time as needed before answering. If the opponent makes a move instead of answering, the response to the draw offer is deemed "no," and the game continues.

475 □ **I**f I offer a draw and my opponent doesn't verbally respond but plays the next move, can my opponent claim a draw at some later point because no answer was given yet?

Once your opponent moves, your draw offer is automatically no longer in effect. Any move equals the response: "No." If the draw offer wasn't annulled by the subsequent move, an opponent could play on and claim a draw whenever loss was imminent.

476 □ Can the players agree to a draw before the game starts?

There would be no chess game if the players could agree to a draw without actually playing. Most tournament directors wouldn't accept it.

Sometimes players in tournaments circumvent officials by secretly agreeing to a draw ahead of time (generally because it enables them both to share a prize without risk), and then playing out a mock game with prearranged moves. Though there's no way to know for sure about such secret agreements, sometimes a tournament director surmises a shady deal and penalizes both participants (with forfeiture or loss of prize money).

477 □ Can I claim a draw by the fifty-move rule without a written score of the game?

You can claim a draw if your claim can be validated. An accurate score is the most dependable method. But if you keep an oral count and it's verified by a tournament director or empowered official, you may be able to claim a draw if fifty moves transpire and if the rules of the given event so allow. Your claim would also stand without an accurate scoresheet or the presence of impartial observers, if your opponent hears the counting and agree with it, but they may not find this approach so agreeable.

478 □ When counting moves for the fifty-move rule, does a White move count as one move and a Black move count as a second move?

A full move consists of a White move and a Black move taken together. If only one side has played a move, that counts as a half move. Therefore, when Black is attempting to draw by the fifty-move rule, it can be claimed just before Black's fiftieth move is played, just before the ensuing argument.

479 □ **W**hy would I want to claim a draw by the fifty-move rule?

If you are losing, the possibility of claiming a draw by the fifty-move rule is one of your last hopes, and half a point is better than nothing. This kind of draw, however, doesn't occur very often in tournament and match games. Usually the stronger side can force checkmate fairly quickly by converting an extra pawn into a queen. Besides, with every pawn move or capture the count must start all over again. But such drawing possibilities do arise and key games have thereby been salvaged, especially in scholastic chess. Stay in school.

480 □ **I**f you use a clock in a tournament game, are you allotted a certain amount of time per move or per game?

Most tournament games require clocks, and time is allotted for the whole game. Each clock should have two timers, one for White and one for Black, and each side's timer has a button that starts one side while stopping the other. Each player is given the same amount of time at the start to complete a certain number of moves, such as two hours for forty moves. This means both White and Black get two hours each to complete their forty moves (forty for White and forty for Black).

A player may use the two hours in whatever way seems fit. A move can be played approximately every three minutes, or the two hours can be used as needed, the player using little time for obvious moves and more time for harder ones. But if one hour and fifty-nine minutes is used for the first move, then only one minute remains to complete the next thirty-nine moves. Good luck.

481 □ **D**uring a tournament, shouldn't I move quickly to save time on the clock if I'm playing an opening variation I know fairly well?

Whenever you can bank clock-time, you should. But what happens if you think you know a position and you really don't? Or if you've confused one position for another? Sometimes your opponent plays a series of moves you've seen before, but varies the order, transposing moves. It could change everything.

Save time whenever you can, but don't be too hasty. Speed isn't everything. Winning is.

482 □ If my opponent is in time trouble, should I play quickly and try to win by a time forfeit?

Quick moves aren't the best way to play against an opponent in time trouble. They increase your own chances of blundering and losing. When you play quickly, you are probably playing obvious moves, the ones your opponent has also considered. On the verge of losing, your opponent's concentration may be a lot more acute than yours.

Instead, use your clock advantage wisely and spend a little thinking time to find solid but unexpected moves and variations. This will force your opponent to consume time analyzing possibilities never anticipated or considered. And if these variations aren't analyzed carefully, your opponent's chances to blunder will surely increase, regardless of the high level of concentration.

483 □ If I can force mate in either two or three moves, and the three-move series is prettier, which should I play, the faster or the prettier mate?

Play the faster one—the fewer moves, the less chance of error. If it's a tournament game, playing the longer mate may cause you to forfeit on time. It's also showy and unprofessional to play unnecessary moves just to impress people. Economy is the artistic hallmark. A shorter mate is almost always more beautiful.

484 □ Why are so many games between grandmasters drawn by agreement?

It's hard to beat a contemporary grandmaster. The game today is played at a sophisticated level where defense and offense are so dynamically balanced that playing for a win entails a considerable element of risk. Since half a point is usually better than no point, there must be an objective reason to play on in many positions. Moreover, many draws are made just to conserve strength for the later rounds in a tournament, especially in those marathon events that drag on for weeks (or, as in the world championship, for months).

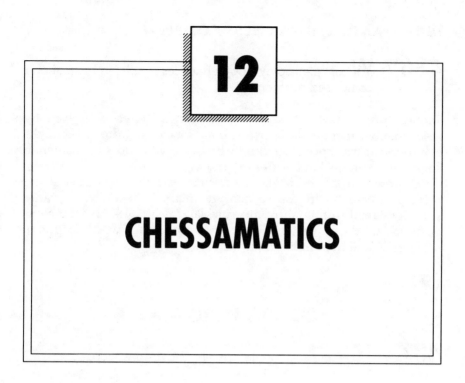

CHESSAMATICS

IT'S MORE THAN A GAME

485 □ **W**hat is the difference between a tactical problem and a composed problem (or composition)?

A tactical problem is a situation that is likely to occur in real chess games. If you play enough chess, you will probably have many opportunities to solve related puzzles. Tactical problems have practical value.

Composed problems can seem almost unreal. They may never occur in any games you will actually play or see. Compositions reflect ideal situations. They are the essence and underlying basis for most real game tactics, but tend to be perfect, with no unnecessary pieces or pawns and every unit on just the right square. Most chess positions have all kinds of unnecessary features, though the essential truths are there.

486 □ **W**hat role is played by principles in solving tactical and composed problems?

Tactical problems (real game situations) can often be solved by resorting to principles as a starting point for investigation. You might ask yourself: What principles apply here? Or, what does the principle suggest I do in this kind of situation?

Composed problems are so particularized that few real game principles could help you to analyze them. In fact, if real game situations tend to follow certain rules and principles, artistic compositions are the opposite. They are more concerned with exceptions to the rule, and therein lies their beauty.

COUNT IT AGAIN

487 □ **H**ow many possible opening moves are there?

There are twenty different moves for beginning a chess game—sixteen pawn moves and four knight moves. Soon thereafter, the possibilities ramify to astronomical numbers. Some analyses give the number of possible chess moves as something like 10 to the 120th power (1 with 120 zeroes after it).

488 □ **H**ow many different ways are there to play a forty-move game?

Hold onto your hat, the number is truly astronomical. It's easy to see that there are twenty different first moves for White and twenty for Black. Multiplying the two together gives four hundred positions that could be reached after each side has played just one move.

According to C. Flye St. Marie's 1895 calculation, 71,852 different legal positions could result after each side has played two moves. This analysis was improved upon by Thomas Dawson (1889–1951) in 1946, increasing the number of actual legal chess positions after the first two moves (based on the order in which they are played) to 72,084.

For three moves, there are about nine million different legal positions, and after that the possible positions ramify to an unbelievable number: there are more different possible forty-move games in chess than all the electrons in the physical universe.

489 □ **H**ow many moves is the longest possible chess game?

I've never seen an indisputable resolution to this question, but the answer is not the millions of moves some experts claim. In a 1938 article in *Chess Review*, chessplayer-mathematician Donald Mac-Murray showed that the longest possible chess game must be somewhat short of 6,237 moves.

In his analysis, if no unit is taken, no pawn advanced, and no checkmate given in fifty moves, the game is drawn by the fifty-move rule. The greatest possible number of captures in a game is thirty (neither king can be captured). Theoretically, the greatest possible number of pawn advances in a game is six for each pawn, making a total of 96. That gives a total of 126 captures and advances (30 plus 96). The longest possible game, therefore, could stretch for 49.5 moves between each two of these advances and captures, and thus could continue for 126 × 49.5, or 6,237 moves. But since some of the captures must be captures of pawns, the actual combined figure for advances and captures must be somewhat less than 126, which means the total number of moves must also be considerably less.

490 □ **H**ow many *en passant* captures are permitted in a game?

No more than eight *en passant* captures are possible, whether one or both sides make them. Each capture must involve both a black pawn and a white pawn, and once a pawn has captured *en passant*, or been captured *en passant*, it can never be in position for either to happen again.

The record for *en passant* captures in a game may be held by Louis Paulsen (1833–91), a leading chess theoretician and world class player in the 1860s and 1870s. He had four *en passant* captures in a game against Adolf Anderssen (1818–79) at Baden–Baden in 1870. (In the actual game, Paulsen had two more possible *en passant* captures but didn't make them.)

491 □ **H**ow many squares are there on a chessboard?

It's a trick question, since the answer depends on your definition of a square. The obvious answer is sixty-four squares, thirty-two light and thirty-two dark. But there are also squares of two-by-two, three-by-three, four-by-four, and so on. Figuring this way, the board offers 204 squares. And if we're interested in undelineated squares, there is an infinite number of them (for example, squares of 1.1 by 1.1, or 3.47 by 3.47, or 2.4673 by 2.4673, etc.)

492 □ What is the "eight queens problem"?

It's a problem of chess pieces rather than of chess. It asks: "Can eight queens be positioned on an otherwise empty chessboard so that no queen is in line to capture any other queen?" The answer is yes, they can. There are actually twelve fundamental solutions and ninety-two positions in all, if you count rotations and reflections.

The underlying pattern consists of two series of four, with consecutive placements in each sequence separated by a knight's move. Using algebraic notation for the squares occupied by a queen, the twelve basic solutions are: (1) a4 b1 c5 d8 e2 f7 g3 h6; (2) a4 b1 c5 d8 e6 f3 g7 h2; (3) a4 b2 c5 d8 e6 f1 g3 h7; (4) a4 b2 c7 d3 e6 f8 g1 h5; (5) a4 b2 c7 d3 e6 f8 g5 h1; (6) a4 b2 c7 d5 e1 f8 g6 h3; (7) a4 b2 c8 d5 e7 f1 g3 h6; (8) a4 b2 c8 d6 e1 f3 g5 h7; (9) a4 b6 c1 d5 e2 f8 g3 h7; (10) a4 b6 c8 d2 e7 f1 g3 h5; (11) a4 b7 c5 d2 e6 f1 g3 h8; and (12) a4 b8 c1 d5 e7 f2 g6 h3.

The origins of the problem are hazy, but it appeared in *Deutsche Schachzeitung* in 1848. Specific solutions had been found in 1850 by the mathematician Johann Gauss (1775–1855) and the astronomer Heinrich Schumacher (1780–1850). The general problem for *n* queens on a square board of *n*×*n* squares was first considered by the mathematician Franz Nauck in 1850. It seems a solution was suggested by Dr. S. Gunther in 1874. His method, relying on determinants, was worked out by Dr. J. W. L. Glaisher later that year.

493 □ On an otherwise empty board, which piece's mobility is not affected by its placement?

The rook. No matter where it's positioned on an empty board, whether in the corner or the middle, it attacks fourteen squares. All the other pieces, the king, queen, bishop, and knight, increase their scope as they approach the center.

A queen in the corner, for example, attacks twenty-one squares but in the center twenty-seven. A knight in the corner observes only two squares but in the center eight. The bishop's mobility varies from a low of seven to a high of thirteen. And even the king improves from a mobility of three in the corner to eight in the middle.

494 □ **A**s an exercise, on an otherwise empty board, how many bishops can be placed so that, regardless of color, no bishop can capture any other bishop?

You can position fourteen bishops so no two occupy the same diagonal. For example, you can fill any row along the edge with eight bishops, none of which attacks another bishop. You can place six more bishops on the opposite edge, leaving the two corner squares unoccupied. None of these six bishops are in position to capture each other or any of the original eight.

495 □ **A**s an exercise, how many knights can be placed on an otherwise empty chessboard so that, regardless of color, no knight is in position to capture any other knight?

The answer is remarkable and elegant. I remember a math textbook years ago that incorrectly gave the answer as twenty-four, and even illustrated the solution, filling up three distant parallel rows with knights (eight knights on the a-file, eight on the d-file, and eight on the h-file). The actual answer is thirty-two! Simply place the knights on squares of the same color. Since knights change the color of the square they occupy each time they move, they can never capture anything occupying the same color square.

496 □ **O**n an otherwise empty board, what is the maximum number of rooks that can be placed so that no rook is in position to capture another?

This is an easy problem to solve: the answer is eight. And if you include reflections and rotations, there are 40,320 ways to do it! (It's eight factorial.) Simply place each rook on a different rank (or different file), making sure none of the rooks occupy the same file (or same rank). An example would be if all the rooks occupied squares on the same long diagonal, either a1-h8 or a8-h1.

The problem can be extended to the most important piece as well. On an otherwise empty board, it's possible to position sixteen kings so none are attacked: for example, on a1, a3, a5, a7, c1, c3, c5, c7, e1, e3, e5, e7, h1, h3, h5, and h7.

13

PUT IN PERSPECTIVE

AGE-OLD PURSUIT

497 □ **W**hat is chess?

As Dr. Samuel Johnson defined it, chess is "a nice and abstruse game in which two sets of puppets are moved in opposition to each other." The true answer to the question, though, depends on who you are, the extent of your puppetry, etc.

To Anatoly Karpov, the twelfth world chess champion, chess is "everything—art, science, sport." José Raoul Capablanca, the third world chess champion, agreed that it was an art and compared chess to "painting or sculpture." Yet painter/sculptor Marcel Duchamp thought it was less art and more of a "violent sport." Henri Poincarè couldn't see its science, nor did fellow mathematician G. H. Hardy, who called it "trivial mathematics." Perhaps with a fuller perspective, mathematician and sporting chess champion Emanuel Lasker didn't classify chess with science or the arts, but saw it as a "struggle" or "fight."

Literary pugilists may have trouble reconciling Sir Walter Scott's calling it a "sad waste of brains" with Johann Wolfgang von Goethe's consideration that it was the "touchstone of the intellect," though maybe not if they've been privy to chess grandmaster/psychoanalyst Reuben Fine's chauvinistic "chess is a contest between two men in which there is considerable ego involvement." This gets close to George Bernard Shaw's defensive denotation of chess as a "foolish expedient for making idle people feel they are doing something very clever." (Shaw stank at chess.) The great Ben Franklin, a chess adept and a sensitive observer, discerned it "wasn't merely an idle amusement," and skilled chess amateur Leo Tolstoy correctly called it "fine entertainment," a view echoed by Isaac Bashevis Singer, who deemed it the "fairest of all games."

Garry Kasparov, the thirteenth champion of the world, clears the air with "chess is battles," for many people see it as a war game. War games form one of the six traditional classifications of board games. The other categories include race games (the oldest known board games, dating back at least five thousand years, in which the object is to get somewhere first), games of position (for example, Japanese Go and tic tac toe), mancala games (big in Africa), games of calculation, and dice games. In war games, victory hinges on capturing, trapping, or destroying. Napoleon, who aspired to checkmate the kings of Europe, thought chess "too difficult to be a game, and not serious enough to be a science or an art."

There's also game theory, which portrays chess quite differently. It's a finite (ends sometime, which is nice to know), two-person (can't be played by the Green Bay Packers), zero sum game (the conqueror gains as much as the vanquished loses), of perfect information (nothing is hidden, everything is capable of being observed by the players, supposedly) and optimal strategy (theoretically, there's a clear approach to maximize your advantages while minimizing your risks).

I myself prefer the more down-to-earth definitions, such as Danish grandmaster Bent Larsen's "chess is a beautiful mistress," or John Maynard Keynes's "a cure for headaches," or Sherlock Holmes's "sign of a scheming mind." These, along with Bobby Fischer's "chess is life," I can put to good use.

498 □ What is the most famous myth on the game's origin?

There are many myths attempting to explain how chess came into existence. In perhaps the best known, a philosopher (usually identified as Sissa, a Brahmin) created the game at the behest of a rich and powerful king. In some tales, the king is despotic and the sage's aim is to teach him a lesson—that he can't rule without the support of his subjects.

In most versions, the king is pleased with the game itself, but annoyed by the wise man's suggested form of reward: a grain of wheat on the chessboard's first square, two grains on the second square, four on the third, eight on on the fourth, and so on, doubling the amount on each square. The monarch, thinking this adds up to practically nothing, tries to persuade the philosopher to accept something more valuable, but fails and relents, ordering the paltry request to be met.

Of course, the reward could not be honored, since the entire wheat supply of the kingdom was quickly exhausted (2^{64}-1, or 18,446,744,073,709,551,615 grains of wheat would be needed). In some accounts, the crafty sage was beheaded, never getting a chance to become a grandmaster.

499 □ Are pawns really "just pawns in the game"?

Pawns are widely used as a symbol connoting expendability and helplessness. Everyman is a pawn against fate and the powers that be.

In chess, though, this is somewhat of a misconception. True, pawns are the least valuable of units and the most often sacrificed. But they do significant work and are an integral part of the whole. Success is impossible without them. As in life, sometimes they are rewarded for their efforts or just get lucky. If they survive to reach the other side, they're transformed into a queen, the most powerful piece of all, though only the second tallest.

500 □ How old is chess?

It's old, all right, but it's probably not as old as the myths claim. A popular misconception purports chess to date back several thousand years B.C. The first documentary evidence we have for it, however, can be traced to 600 A.D., when it was mentioned in various Indian and Persian sources. Several recent archaelogical discoveries (apparent game parts resembling chess pieces) may take it back to the second century A.D., but these are somewhat questionable.

Most authorities believe chess is a descendant of chataranga, a game played in western India, probably no earlier than 450 A.D., if indeed that early.

A number of games, more ancient than chataranga, shared some of the characteristics of chess, but only chataranga offered all five of the following: (1) it was played on an eight-by-eight-square board, usually with alternating light and dark squares; (2) it used units of different colors, powers, shapes, and sizes; (3) it empowered units to capture each other, rather than just displace each other; (4) it concluded when a particular unit was captured and/or rendered immobile; and (5) it didn't necessarily require the throw of dice (chataranga could be played with or without them).

In these essentials, chataranga qualifies as the first real strategy game and is generally regarded as the forerunner of chess. But we welcome any real evidence of an earlier origin.

501 □ What were the pieces like in chataranga?

The chataranga units paralleled segments of the Indian army of the time. The pieces represented real war counterparts, and to some extent, imitated those counterparts by the way they moved.

The *Ratha* or "chariot" (in some cases this was a *Roka* or "boat") moved up and down or across and was positioned in the corner. It would become the rook in chess. The *Asva* or "horse" became the knight, with movement exactly like today's knight (it's remained unchanged in fourteen centuries). The *Gaja* or "elephant" moved to any of five squares, one to either side of it and the three adjacent squares on the row in front of it. The five possible moves represented a combination of the elephant's four limbs and trunk. The *Gaja* would later become the bishop. The *Padati* or "infantryman" moved one square forward, and in chess became the pawn. Then there was the *Mantri* or "counsellor," a weak piece moving only one square diagonally ahead, and the *Rajah* or "king," which moved one square in any direction, as does the modern king.

502 □ Was chataranga played by two players or four?

It's uncertain, but it appears that chataranga (meaning "four-membered" or "four-armed") was originally a contest between two players, as is chess. Much later, it became a four-player game called chaturaja, meaning "four kings."

In the four-player game, each participant's forces occupied a separate corner of the same sixty-four-square board used in the two-player game. In some versions of chaturaja, it's likely that players teamed up, with one's partner occupying the corner diagonally across the board. Each side (Black, Red, Green, and Yellow, for example) started with eight units: a king, a rook, a bishop, a knight, and four pawns. Thus, two-player teams actually had a total of sixteen units at their combined disposal, with two kings and no queen. If your partner's king was lost, you would assume the remaining forces.

503 □ When was the first international tournament held?

The first such event was held in 1851 at the Great Exhibition in London, with sixteen players competing in the top section of a knockout tournament. In the first round, the matches consisted of three games, but subsequent rounds included matches of seven games, the winner being the first player to score four points. The tournament was eventually won by German mathematician Adolf Anderssen (1818–79), who afterward was considered the best player in the world. Anderssen won four head-to-head matchups impressively, defeating in order Lionel Adelberto Bagration Felix Kieseritzky (1806–53); Joszef Szen (1805–57); Howard Staunton (1810–74), then unofficial world champion; and Marmaduke Wyvill (1814–96), who took second place.

ROLL CALL OF CHAMPIONS

504 □ How many world champions have emerged since the title became official?

We've had thirteen world champions since 1886, when the first official championship match was held between Steinitz and Zukertort. Their title years and country of origin were: (1) Wilhelm Steinitz (1886–94, Austria); (2) Emanuel Lasker (1894–1921, Germany); (3) José Raoul Capablanca (1921–27, Cuba); (4) Alexander Alekhine (1927–35 and 1937–46, Russia); (5) Max Euwe (1935–37, Holland); (6) Mikhail Botvinnik (1948–57, 1958–60, and 1961–63, Soviet Union); (7) Vassily Smyslov (1957–58, Soviet Union); (8) Mikhail Tal (1960–61, Soviet Union); (9) Tigran Petrosian (1963–69, Soviet Union); (10) Boris Spassky (1969–72, Soviet Union); (11) Bobby Fischer (1972–75, United States); (12) Anatoly Karpov (1975–85, Soviet Union); (13) Garry Kasparov (1985 to present, Soviet Union). Since 1927, Russians (Soviet or expatriate) have held the title in all but five years.

505 □ Why are the Russians so good at chess?

The Soviet government had always taken the game seriously. Indeed, it's known that Lenin and Trotsky, and other leading Bolsheviks, were avid chessplayers.

The initial impetus was provided by A. F. Ilyin–Zhenevsky (1894–1941) in 1924, who convinced the party to integrate the development of chess into the overall plan. Ilyin–Zhenevsky won approval by arguing that the pastime brought out mental qualities valuable to a soldier: "boldness, presence of mind, composure, a strong will, and, most important, a sense of strategy." In short, the Soviets backed it mainly because it seemed to have military significance, and only secondarily to show that Marxism–Leninism produces greater intellects.

The organizing reins were handed to N. V. Krylenko (1885–1938), who was an extremely important figure in the early years of the Soviet regime (he was appointed commander-in-chief of the Russian forces after the October Revolution). He also became head of the Chess Section of the Supreme Council for Physical Culture, with the job of disseminating the nation's chess program.

How the gospel was spread was captured in the memoirs of international master Fedor Ivanovich Dus–Khotimirsky (1879–1965): "Soon the central chess section enrolled me to carry out this work in the provinces. During the next seven years, from 1924 to 1931, I travelled through almost the entire Soviet Union—from the White Sea to the Caucasus, from the Baltic to Vladivostok—passing on my experience and knowledge to the young people of eight Soviet republics, the Ukraine, White Russia, Uzbekistan, Kazakhstan, Turkmenia, Georgia, Armenia and Azerbaidzhan. I visited dozens of towns, putting out propaganda on behalf of chess, organizing chess sections on physical culture committees and chess columns in the local press, giving lectures and simultaneous displays, taking part in republic and city championships, training individual players and bringing on groups of youngsters."

It's clear why chess in the U.S.S.R. succeeded: because of programs like the above, because of financial and official support, and in consequence, because of the high esteem the public had for the game. Individuals responded by devoting their lives to chess.

506 □ When was the first official world championship match held and who emerged as the first world champion?

Pity the poor unsung world champions of yore! Various confrontations were recognized as unofficial world championships, at least as far back as the mid-fifteen hundreds. But who remembers them?

The first match accepted and heralded as an official world championship encounter occurred in 1886 between Wilhelm Steinitz of Austria and Johannes Zukertort of Germany. Steinitz won the match, which consisted of twenty games, with a score of ten wins, five draws, and five losses. It was held in three U.S. cities, starting January 11 in New York, where the first five games were played. Games six through nine were contested in St. Louis, and the final eleven games were fought in New Orleans, the last game ending on March 29, 1886.

507 □ Which player has the highest winning percentage in world championship encounters?

Emanuel Lasker (1868–1941) scored 64.7 percent through seven world championship matches and one hundred two games. He won forty-five games, drew forty-two, and lost only fifteen against the world's best. The second highest winning percentage (59.5) was achieved by Bobby Fischer (born 1943), who played only one title match, defeating Boris Spassky in 1972 by a score of seven wins, eleven draws, and three losses.

508 □ What was the longest world championship match of all time?

From September 10, 1984, to February 15, 1985 (one hundred fifty-nine days), Anatoly Karpov and Garry Kasparov played forty-eight games in Moscow. After the forty-eighth game, the match was stopped by Florencio Campomanes, the president of FIDE (The World Chess Federation), citing exhaustion of the players and organizers. At that point Karpov was leading by a score of five to three, with forty draws, though Kasparov had won the last two games and seemed to be on a roll when Mr. Campomanes halted the festivities. Since the title was to be awarded to the first player to win six games, and no one had done this, the match ended with no decision, Karpov retaining his title, which he lost to Kasparov in a return match (September 3 to November 9, 1985).

In terms of games, however, Karpov–Kasparov (1984–85) wasn't the longest match ever contested between the world's two top players. That record is shared by Louis Charles de la Bourdonnais of France (1795–1840) and Alexander McDonnell of England (1798–1835). In 1834, from June to October, they played six matches, totaling eighty-five games, which history has generally regarded as one match. La

Bourdonnais won the unofficial world championship by an overall score of forty-five wins, twenty-seven losses, and thirteen draws.

509 ▫ Who was the oldest person ever to win a world championship match?

In 1892, Wilhelm Steinitz (1836–1900) of Austria, the first official champion, retained his title in a match against Mikhail Chigorin (1850–1908) of Russia. The then 56-year-old Steinitz won by a score of ten to eight, with five draws.

510 ▫ Who was the youngest person ever to win a world championship match?

In a match played from September 3, 1985, to November 9, 1985, Garry Kasparov of the Soviet Union defeated his countryman Anatoly Karpov by a score of five to three, with sixteen draws. Kasparov was still twenty-two years old at the match's conclusion, having been born on April 13, 1963.

511 ▫ Who was the youngest U.S. champion of all time?

Bobby Fischer, the "boy from Brooklyn," won the first of his eight national championships in early 1958 (for the year 1957–58) when he was still fourteen years old. Fischer went on to capture the world championship in 1972, defeating Boris Spassky of the Soviet Union by a score of seven wins and three losses (two actual losses and one forfeit), with eleven draws.

512 ▫ What is the highest international title a chessplayer can hold?

If we don't include world champion, a distinction held by only one person at a time, grandmaster is the highest title that FIDE (the Fédération Internationale des Échecs) awards. It's earned by achieving certain scores (norms) in at least several FIDE-sanctioned events and through a specified number of games. The title was introduced officially in 1950, though it had been used informally to describe the game's elite as far back as François-Andre Danican Philidor (1726–95), the strongest player of the eighteenth century.

513 □ Who was the youngest person ever to win the grand-master title?

Until early 1992, the youngest grandmaster of all time was Robert James Fischer (better known as Bobby) of the United States, who earned the distinction in 1958 at the age of fifteen. Fischer was born on March 9, 1943, in Chicago. However, Judit Polgar now has that distinction. At fifteen years, four months and twenty-seven days, she is the youngest grandmaster ever, eclipsing Fischer's record of fifteen years, six months, and one day.

514 □ What factors in young children suggest talent for chess?

No conclusive studies have been done in this area, and speculation is rife. In my own experience, many of the children who eventually developed into good chessplayers generally displayed a range of abilities and propensities. But they had some things in common, too.

One sign is eye movement while at the board. If there's a lot of it, the child is undoubtedly thinking, considering chess moves by picturing them in the mind's eye. Since young children, in particular, tend to stare at the board after a short time, a child exhibiting continual eye movement will stand out immediately. It doesn't matter if the child's actual ideas are correct; it's the thought process itself that's important.

Other common attributes include: (1) a long attention span and the ability to follow through on a certain point, question, or line of reasoning; (2) a love of problem solving and game playing; (3) the will to win, a positive obstinacy, a need to prove a point by reason or until achieving success; and (4) a general facility for doing things mentally.

This last point is critical. Chess requires that you see the consequences of your moves ahead of time, which means you need a good imagination. The most creative young chessplayers often have a rich fantasy life in which they work out entire scenarios and plots, starring themselves as hero. Some youngsters will play over all the winner's games from a tournament, pretending to be that player while the moves are reviewed on a practice chessboard.

Of course, talent isn't the only key to early chess interest and success. At least equally significant is parental involvement. If the parents think the game is important, so will the child.

515 □ Who was the greatest chess prodigy?

Most people would opt for Bobby Fischer. But when I think of prodigies, I have in mind those who displayed skilled, adultlike performance before the age of ten. By his own admission, Fischer didn't "get good" until he was thirteen.

In the history of chess, two real prodigies stand out: José Raoul Capablanca (1888–1942) and Samuel Reshevsky (1911–92). Other authorities add Paul Morphy (1837–84) to this list, but though he may have been outstanding before the age of twelve, the factual evidence on Morphy is inconclusive. There have been many other young talents who developed before the age of ten (such as all the recent world champions), but on paper none of them quite match Capablanca or Reshevsky.

If we jump to the age of twelve, however, you'd have to give serious consideration to the Hungarian *wunderkind* Judit Polgar, who was born in 1976. In 1988, she achieved an Elo rating of 2550, the highest ever for that age. In a head-on adolescent match against either Capa or Sammy, my money would be on Judit.

516 □ Is it true that women don't play chess as well as men?

I wish this question would go away, but it rears up almost every time I give a talk. It's true the best players in the world have always been men. Maybe boys traditionally are permitted more opportunities to be competitive and aggressive, or it may be that parental, social, and institutional biases grant boys more impactful experience with critical thinking techniques, or perhaps society has decided it's a male's game, and that's that.

I was particularly confronted by this question when in 1982 I was a consultant on Walter Tevis's book *The Queen's Gambit*. The main character of the book, an eight-year-old girl named Beth Harmon, is a chess genius who, as the title implies, goes on to become the best player in the world. Walter (and Random House) was greatly concerned that the premise might be too implausible, though he personally believed it could happen.

Having worked with numerous youngsters, I knew firsthand it was entirely reasonable. In fact, before the age of six, talented girls and boys are chessically indistinguishable.

But something happens at six, and a greater percentage of boys start to get more involved. Perhaps, as a few scientists assert, it has to do with the right and left halves of the brain and their corresponding neural patterns. Or probably, as most children's chess teachers believe, it's simply the cumulative weight of societal pressures, which finally begin to take effect. I don't really know what to say. I'm sure Judit Polgar does.

517 □ What is the hypermodern school of chess?

The term hypermodern was coined by Dr. Saviely Tartakower (1887–1956) in the 1920s. He referred to a movement spearheaded by Aron Nimzovich (1886–1935) and Richard Reti (1889–1929), which was opposed to the traditional approaches to playing for the center.

Standard theory held that one should occupy the center early on, but hypermodernists emphasized trying to control the center before actually occupying it. They advocated flank bishop developments and pawn advances just off the center, or even pawn advances on the flank issuing indirect central attacks. Chess theory assimilated these ideas, and now hypermodern concepts are weapons in every grandmaster's arsenal.

WHO'S WHO

518 □ Who was Tarrasch?

Dr. Siegbert Tarrasch (1862–1934) was a German grandmaster ranked among the world's top players for at least two decades. He lost a world championship match to Emanuel Lasker in 1908.

Tarrasch is perhaps best known for his teachings, which stressed open lines, development, mobility (especially), and centrally based play, at the expense of pawn structure and other intangibles. For example, he was willing to accept an isolated pawn—a potentially long-term weakness—if it led to greater immediate activity for his pieces.

He was a very influential writer, revered for his annotated collections of games and his 1931 textbook, *Das Schachspiel*, which was translated into English in 1935 as *The Game of Chess*.

519 □ Who was Nimzovich?

Aron Nimzovich, born in Riga, Latvia, on November 7, 1886, was one of the strongest players of the 1920s (at one time ranked third in the world behind Capablanca and Alekhine). He is considered the founder of the hypermodern movement in chess, an integral part of contemporary theory and practice.

Nimzovich's ideas were expounded in three seminal books: *Die Blockade* (1925), translated into English in 1980 as *Blockade*; *Mein System* (1925), which many regard as the greatest of all chess books, translated into English as *My System* in 1929; and *Die Praxis meines Systems* (1929), translated into English as *Chess Praxis* in 1936.

520 □ Who was Reti?

Richard Reti (1889–1929) was one of the founders of the hypermodern school of chess, along with Aron Nimzovich (1886–1935), Alexander Alekhine (1892–1946), Yefim Bogolyubov (1889–1952), Gyula Breyer (1894–1921), Saviely Tartakower (1887–1956), and Ernst Grünfeld (1893–1962). With them he invigorated opening play by finding new ways to fight for the center and control the initiative, essentially as a reaction to the dogmatic teachings of Siegbert Tarrasch (1862–1934).

Grandmaster Reti, a Hungarian by birth, and later a Czech, is equally known for his endgame studies and other original contributions to endgame theory, and also for the opening bearing his name, the Reti Opening (which is begun by White's first-move development of the king-knight to f3).

Reti also wrote two classic books: *Die neuen Ideen in Schachspiel* (1922), republished in English as *Modern Ideas in Chess* (1923); and *Die Meister des Schachbretts* (1930), which was modified and subsequently published in English as *Masters of the Chess Board* (1933). It's in these books that Reti propounds his evolutionary theory of chess, in which he asserts, drawing upon a doctrine popular in other disciplines, that the development of the individual chessplayer recapitulates the evolution of chess theory.

521 □ Who was Marshall?

Frank James Marshall (1877–1944), an American grandmaster, was one of the world's top ten players for about twenty years, from 1904 to 1925. He won the U.S. championship in 1909, claiming the title after defeating Jackson Showalter (1860–1935) in a match by the score of seven to two, with three draws. He defended his title only once, in 1924 against Edward Lasker (five to four, with nine draws), and retained it until 1936, when he surrendered it by announcing his intention not to play in America's first championship tournament, which was won by Samuel Reshevsky. A speculative and fantastic attacking player, he will always be remembered for his spirited combinations and the chess club he founded in New York's Greenwich Village, which still bears his name.

522 □ Who was Reshevsky?

Samuel Herman Reshevsky (1911–92), better known as Sammy, was born in Poland. He learned the game at the age of four, became a strong player by the age of six, when he toured the country giving exhibitions, and by eight was conducting successful blindfold simultaneouses.

Reshevsky came to the U.S. in 1920 and became a citizen. He went on to a distinguished career, triumphing in numerous international events and winning the U.S. championship on six occasions. At one time he was ranked as high as third in the world, but never had the opportunity to play a match for the world championship.

523 □ Who is Fine?

Dr. Reuben Fine (born in 1914), is an American grandmaster and a leading Freudian psychoanalyst, and at one time was ranked among the top six players in the world. His greatest chess achievement was tying for first, with Paul Keres (1916–75) of Estonia, in the 1938 AVRO tournament, regarded by authorities as one of the game's historic tournaments. The other six combatants, all among the game's elite, included four world champions—Alexander Alekhine (1892–1946), José Raoul Capablanca (1888–1942), Mikhail Botvinnik (born 1911), and Max Euwe (1901–81)—and two outstanding players: Fine's long-time rival Samuel Reshevsky (1911–92), and the positional artist Salo Flohr (1908–83).

In 1948 Fine opted not to compete in the world championship tournament, essentially retiring from chess to pursue a career as a practicing psychoanalyst. A prolific writer, Dr. Fine has given the world a number of valuable and interesting books, including the indispensable classic *Basic Chess Endings* (1941) and the controversial *The Psychology of the Chessplayer* (1956).

524 □ Who was Loyd?

Sam Loyd (1841–1911), "the puzzle king," created interesting chess problems and was also quite possibly the most gifted American puzzle maker. His diversions and problems (not just those on chess) are enjoyed and respected worldwide. In addition to chess puzzles, Sam Loyd composed crosswords, riddles, rebuses, conundrums, constructions, logic problems, and the like.

One of his better-known creations was the 15–14 puzzle, which is a four-by-four square frame containing fifteen small numbered squares, with one space free to allow shifting of the other squares. The squares were arranged in numerical order except that the 14 and 15 were out of order. The idea was to switch the 14 and 15 while keeping the others in correct order. As many solvers soon found out, the problem had no solution. It was Loyd who also reintroduced the ancient game of Parchesi (originally Pachisi) in the late 18th century. Many of his puzzles and curious pastimes can be found in Martin Gardner's *Mathematical Puzzles of Sam Loyd* (1958) and *More Mathematical Puzzles of Sam Loyd* (1960).

Regarding his chess problems, Loyd's philosophy was to achieve an artistic effect by posing situations in which the answer was supposedly the least likely possibility (after seeing the solution you'd say "aha!"). Most of Loyd's chess problems appear in A. C. White's *Sam Loyd and his Chess Problems* (1913).

525 □ Who was Philidor?

François-Andre Danican Philidor (1726–95) was the best chessplayer of the eighteenth century, and perhaps the first really good player in history. He was a musical composer of considerable repute, having developed the comic opera. Philidor wrote the most influential chess book of his time, *L'analyse du jeu des Échecs*, in which he expounded the idea that "pawns are the soul of chess." Among the concepts named after this eminent Frenchman are: Philidor's draw, a drawing technique in rook endings; Philidor's legacy, a kind of smothered mate; and Philidor's defense, an opening system for Black.

526 □ Who was Morphy?

Paul Morphy (1837–84) of New Orleans was the world's strongest player from 1858 to 1863. He's credited with invigorating the game by the force of his brilliant attacks and total-command play.

Though Morphy wouldn't compare to today's leading grandmasters in absolute strength, some observers feel he was, in relative terms, the strongest player of all time, the argument being that Morphy was further ahead of his generation than any other top player has been ahead of his. Referred to as "the pride and sorrow of chess," Morphy has come to symbolize the tragic artist who, on the verge of great achievement, self-destructs.

527 □ Who was Steinitz?

Wilhelm Steinitz (1836–1900), an Austrian born in Prague, was the first official world champion, a title he claimed in 1886 after defeating Johann Hermann Zukertort (1842–88). Steinitz won the match, held in New York, St. Louis, and New Orleans by a score of ten to five, with five draws.

Most authorities acknowledge that Steinitz was the world's top player from 1866, when he won a match from Adolf Anderssen (1818–79), to 1894, when he lost a match (the first match loss of his life) to Emanuel Lasker (1868–1941).

Steinitz was a tenacious fighter, who played every game for blood and wrote about chess with passionate abandon. In his games and writings he developed the theory of positional play, the foundation of today's chess, and is universally considered the game's seminal teacher.

528 □ Who was Emanuel Lasker?

Emanuel Lasker (1868–1941), not to be confused with his German-born American distant cousin, the international master Edward Lasker (1885–1981), was the second world champion of chess, winning the title from Steinitz in 1894 by a score of ten to five, with four draws. He held the title for twenty-seven years, finally losing it to Capablanca in 1921 in Havana.

In addition to his championship matches, Lasker, a mathematician by profession, won both the 1914 St. Petersburg and 1924 New York tournaments, ahead of his two chief rivals, Capablanca and Alekhine. He was a complete player, but especially dangerous in defense and counterattack, often luring his opponents into unsound sacrifices and then refuting them with deadly accuracy in the middlegame and endgame, of which he was the nonpareil master.

529 □ Who was Capablanca?

José Raoul Capablanca (1888–1942) was the third chess champion of the world, a title he took from Emanuel Lasker by a score of four to zero, with ten draws, in a match held in Havana, Cuba, in 1921. Known as the Invincible Capablanca, he lost fewer tournament and match games (thirty-five) than any other player, at one point losing only one game in eight years.

A remarkable prodigy, Capablanca learned chess at the age of four merely by watching his father play. He developed a flawless technique, not unlike Fischer's, which often seemed to give his winning play an inevitability. Remarkably, he lost the title in his first defense of it, in 1927 in Buenos Aires, Argentina, to Alekhine; the score was six to three, with twenty-five draws. He was never able to obtain a return match, which many authorities feel he would have won. To this day Capablanca remains the game's symbol of perfection.

530 □ Who was Alekhine?

Russian-born Alexander Alekhine (1892–1946) was the fourth champion of the world, holding the title from 1927, when he defeated José Raoul Capablanca, to 1935, when he lost to Max Euwe; and again from 1937, when he regained the title by beating Euwe, until his death in 1946. He was the only champion to die while holding the title.

A powerful, creative, and feared player, Alekhine was respected in all phases of the game, though he is perhaps most remembered for his deep combinations, some of which are incredibly profound. He had few equals as a writer, and his various books are collectively considered the most revealing works by a top-level player.

531 □ Who was Euwe?

Max Euwe (1901–81), whose last name is pronounced "erver," not "yoo" or "yoowee," as some fans say, was the fifth official world chess champion. No one believed he had a chance to beat Alekhine in 1935, but Euwe managed to play great chess and opportunely usurped the title by a single game. Two years later, he lost the return match and Alekhine was again champ.

Stylistically, Euwe was a master of lively positions, with pieces in conflict across the board. He was a gentleman and a sporting champion, qualities that led to his election as president of the World Chess Federation 1970–78, the only world champion ever to hold that position.

532 □ **W**ho is Botvinnik?

Mikhail Botvinnik (born 1911), was the sixth world chess champion, a title he assumed by winning the 1948 Hague–Moscow tournament, held to determine a new champion after the death of Alekhine. Botvinnik kept the title until 1957, when he lost to Smyslov. He regained it a year later, then lost it to Tal in 1960, and won it back in 1961. Finally, he lost to Petrosian in 1963 and decided to stop competing.

Often called the founder of the Soviet school, Botvinnik excelled in complex strategical positions requiring dynamic breakthroughs. He is famed for his meticulous development of whole new opening systems, charting them well into the middlegame. Like Alekhine, he is a first-rate writer, and his game collections have inspired generations of chessplayers. Two of those who learned from him, Garry Kasparov and Anatoly Karpov, did okay.

533 □ **W**ho is Smyslov?

The seventh world chess champion, Vassily Smyslov (born 1921), learned how to play in his father's library at the age of six. He developed rapidly, and was eventually recognized as the second greatest Soviet player in the 1940s, right behind Mikhail Botvinnik. He played three world championship matches with Botvinnik, drawing in 1954, winning in 1957, and losing in 1958. All told, he won the 69-game series by a single game!

A finished master of all phases of chess, Smyslov was a great opening innovator with a flowing, logical middlegame and a total command of the endgame. His *Rook Endings*, which he co-authored with Grigory Levenfish (1889–1961), is acknowledged as the standard work in the field.

534 □ **W**ho is Tal?

When Mikhail Tal (born 1936) captured the title from Botvinnik in 1960, he became the youngest world champion ever up to that point. But he lost the title back to Botvinnik a year later, and never managed to challenge for it again.

Throughout his life the eighth world chess champion has suffered from chronic health problems, which have led to erratic play. When he's up, he's respected as a deep tactical player, who unleashes sequences of surprise combinations and brilliant sacrifices which usually can't be analyzed over the board—the kind spectators love and opponents fear.

535 □ Who was Petrosian?

The ninth world champion, Tigran Petrosian (1929–84) is probably one of the least appreciated title-holders, his moves often seeming obscure and even irrational. But the logic was always there, and so was the artistry which made him a truly unique champion.

Petrosian was a positional genius, a consummate endgame specialist, and a true master of the closed game, with the uncanny ability to find labyrinthine maneuvers and profound "prevent defenses." He held the title for six years, taking it from Botvinnik in 1963 and losing it to Spassky in 1969.

536 □ Who is Spassky?

Boris Spassky, the tenth world champion, was born on January 30, 1937, in Leningrad, Soviet Union. He won the world junior championship in 1955 (in Antwerp), was awarded the grandmaster title the same year, and captured the world championship in 1969, defeating Tigran Petrosian (1929–84) by a score of six to four, with thirteen draws. His name was indelibly etched into the pages of chess history when he lost his 1972 world championship defense, held in Reykjavik, Iceland, to Bobby Fischer. To this day, that match is still considered the greatest chess showdown ever.

537 □ Who is Fischer?

Robert James Fischer, known as Bobby, the eleventh world champion and the only native American to win the title, was born in Chicago on March 9, 1943. At the age of six, in Brooklyn, New York, where Fischer lived most of his youth, he was first taught to play chess by his sister, Joan, and a nearby chess teacher, Carmine Nigro.

His achievements are legendary, including winning the U.S. championship eight times, starting at the age of fourteen, making him the youngest champion ever; becoming the youngest grandmaster ever at fifteen in 1958 (surpassed by Judit Polgar in 1992); winning two interzonal tournaments (1962 and 1970); being the only player to shut out the field in a U.S. championship (eleven to zero in 1963–64); winning twenty consecutive games in international competition, including shutting out two top grandmasters in candidates matches for the world championship, both by six to zero scores (Russia's Mark Taimanov and Denmark's Bent Larsen, both in 1971); and in 1972 winning the world title from Russia's Boris Spassky by a score of seven to three with eleven draws.

Before his match with Spassky, Fischer had the highest Elo rating of all time at 2785 (since surpassed by Kasparov's 2800 in 1990). Some authorities still consider him, when at his peak, the strongest chessplayer in history.

538 □ **W**ho is Karpov?

Anatoly Karpov, the twelfth world champion, was born on May 23, 1951, in Zlatoust, Soviet Union. He was awarded the title in 1975 when Bobby Fischer opted not to defend it in a championship match. Karpov thereby became only the second world champion to assume the title without having defeated the previous champion in a match. (Botvinnik was the first.)

Karpov proved to be an outstanding world champion, winning many first prizes in international tournaments and holding the championship for ten years before losing it to Kasparov in 1985. Behind Kasparov, he is generally regarded as the number two active player.

539 □ **W**ho is Kasparov?

Garry Kasparov, the thirteenth and youngest world champion, was born on April 13, 1963, in Baku, Azerbaidzhan. He was world junior champion in 1980, and became world champion in 1985, defeating Anatoly Karpov in a title match by the score of five to three, with sixteen draws.

All told, as of 1991, he has had five matches with his nemesis Karpov. The first, in 1984, was annulled with Karpov leading by two points, though Kasparov seemed on the verge of turning the match. The second and third matches (1985 and 1986) were won by Kasparov; the fourth (1987) was drawn when Kasparov saved the day by winning the last game; and the fifth (1990), played half in New York and half in Lyons, was won by Kasparov.

He is the highest rated player of all time, aspiring to 2800 on the Elo list in 1990, and has brought a renascence to the game with his brilliant play, dynamic personality, and formidable presence. Whether he's debating world leaders on human rights, verbally sparring on the David Letterman Show, or playing for the first prize in the last round of a major chess tournament, he's a tough man to beat.

540 □ Who was the best chessplayer of all time?

This question can be answered in a number of ways, depending on the selected criteria.

We could say that the current champion is best because, as in other disciplines, history confers on him an advantage in perspective. Conversely, we could advocate as best the discoverers of new ideas and approaches—the original pioneers and groundbreakers—and argue that those who came afterward are mere followers or copycats. If they play with more finesse, what of it? They have an undeniable advantage.

Other criteria for judging the best are ratings (whose Elo is highest); longevity (who reigned the longest); the closeness of the nearest competitor (who was furthest ahead of his contemporaries); success at the top (who had the highest winning percentage in individual match-ups with his nearest rivals); courage (who took the biggest risks by playing in the most dangerous events while champion); and simple tournament and match results (who won the most first prizes).

Nor, if we are realists, could we exclude subjective considerations. It would be fatuous to ignore a champion's quality of play, technique, creativity, artistry, depth, and overall contributions to theory.

After weighing everything, today's tendency is to lean toward Garry Kasparov, the current world champion. His 2800 Elo rating, achieved in 1990, was the highest ever recorded. As the reigning king, Kasparov also benefits from his historical vantage point and from his access to state-of-the-art literature and training methods, such as the use of computers. Moreover, he's won almost every major event in which he's participated, including some of the strongest tournaments ever held, and he's never backed down from a challenge. He plays the best and beats them.

Other authorities argue in favor of Anatoly Karpov, especially during his ten-year dominance, 1975–85. During this period, Karpov, like Kasparov later on, won every major tournament in which he competed and successfully fended off several challenges to his crown. And even though Kasparov has clearly bested Karpov in their five head-to-head matches, Karpov was never routed. His supporters might reasonably argue that the younger Karpov would have been even more formidable.

But what about the redoubtable Bobby Fischer? Rather than losing his title in 1975, he simply surrendered it, refusing to defend it in a dispute with FIDE. For three years, 1970–72, Fischer had no peer, winning matches by unheard of scores (six to zero vs. Mark Taimanov, six to zero vs. Bent Larsen, and six and a half to two and a half vs. Tigran Petrosian), capping it with a convincing defeat of Boris Spassky in their 1972 world championship match in Reykjavik, Iceland. Fischer's final Elo rating of 2780 (before the Spassky match he was 2785) is not so far from Kasparov's 2800 that Bobby couldn't have added to his rating and maintained his superiority, especially with the incentive of knowing that one day Kasparov would catch up and pass him.

The same argument holds for José Raoul Capablanca, who lost only one game in eight years and was characterized as invincible. Capa often agreed to draw games he could have won, particularly if it didn't jeopardize his tournament standing, something that Kasparov and Fischer never would do. If Capablanca had known that retroactively (fifty years later!) he would be rated for these games (there was no rating system in his day) and would thereby be ranked lower than subsequent world champions, he might have increased his rating significantly.

Somehow we have to deal with the player who beat Capablanca—Alexander Alekhine. He was awesome in every aspect of the game. After winning the title from Capablanca in Buenos Aires in 1927, for five years he was just as unbeatable as Capa. More textbook examples are drawn from his chess than from that of any other grandmaster, and it's impossible to exclude him from serious discussions of the game's best, despite his objectionable political beliefs. Even Kasparov has admired Alekhine's genius.

We could also add to our list three other outstanding figures: Mikhail Botvinnik, the driving force behind the Soviet school, who for twenty years (1940–60) was the world's best player; Emanuel Lasker, a tough-minded survivor, who held the title for twenty-seven years (1894–1921), far longer than any other official title-holder; and Wilhelm Steinitz, the first official world champion and the game's most important teacher, who for many years stood alone atop the chess pantheon.

We must not forget the almost legendary Paul Morphy. The American whirlwind of the late 1850s and early 1860s never played an official match for the world championship, but some authorities believe he was the relative best, since he displayed the greatest superiority over his nearest rivals, crushing Adolf Anderssen (1818–79) and every other top competitor he met.

So we're back where we started. On what basis do we determine the game's best player? Probably a majority of commentators would say it's Kasparov, with reasonable grounds to support the contention. In an absolute sense he is far stronger than Morphy or Steinitz, although not truly in a relative sense. Still there are those who say it's Fischer. All chess fans lament that Bobby never played Anatoly or Garry.

541 □ Who are the best American players?

If we're talking historically, I'll go out on the limb and say Paul Morphy (1837–1884), George Mackenzie (1837–1891), Harry Nelson Pillsbury (1872–1906), Frank Marshall (1877–1944), Samuel Reshevsky (1911–1992), Reuben Fine (born 1914), Bobby Fischer (born 1943), Walter Browne (born 1949), Yasser Seirawan (born 1960), and Gata Kamsky (born 1975). I would also include Isaac Kashdan (1905–1985), Arnold Denker (born 1914), Robert Byrne (born 1928), Pal Benko (born 1928), Arthur Bisguier (born 1929), Larry Evans (born 1932), Bill Lombardy (born 1937), and Lubosh Kavalek (born 1943).

A fair representation of contemporary American playing strength is the roster from the 1991 U.S. Championship. In addition to Gata Kamsky, the current champion, it includes fellow New Yorkers Lev Alburt, Joel Benjamin, Roman Dzindzichashvili, and John Fedorowicz; from New Jersey, Maxim Dlugy, Boris Gulko, Michael Rohde, and Alex Yermolinsky; from California, Walter Browne and Igor Ivanov; from Massachusetts, Ilya Gurevich, Alexander Ivanov, and Patrick Wolff; Sergei Kudrin from Connecticut and Yasser Seirawan from Washington. And though he didn't compete in this event, Larry Christiansen of New York, perennially one of our strongest players, must also be recognized.

Finally, it makes sense to list the top ten players under sixteen years old on the annual 1991 USCF rating list: New Yorkers Stanislav Garber, Erez Klein, Boris Kreiman, Joshua Waitzkin, and Jorge Zamora; Danny Benjamin (Pennsylvania), Michael Manion (Wisconsin), Michael Molyar (Colorado), Paul Rohwer (Nebraska), and Tal Shaked (Arizona).

542 □ Will Fischer ever play again?

I also get questions about what happened to Bobby, where he is, why he quit, and whether he would have beaten Kasparov and Karpov. Taking all the variants as a single block, they constitute by far the most often asked questions at talks and lectures. I don't think I've ever made a public presentation without hearing someone inquire about America's charismatic, elusive chess genius.

As of the time of this writing (late 1992), Bobby Fischer has not played a single public game since winning the world championship in 1972. There have been many rumors about possible matches since, but nothing has yet materialized. Perhaps if the conditions are right, Fischer will again enter the arena. Until then, the world must be content with reliving the hundreds of masterpieces he left us.

543 □ Who was Reinfeld?

Fred Reinfeld (1910–64) was the most prolific chess writer ever, purportedly having produced more than two hundred books, including some on subjects other than chess, such as coin and stamp collecting. A founder in 1933 of *Chess Review,* with Al Horowitz and Isaac Kashdan, Reinfeld's name is known the world over as a master explicator of chess concepts and arcana, and indeed his publications have introduced millions of newcomers to the fold.

544 □ How does a computer decide on its moves?

The first program that laid a foundation for the basic algorithms of computer chess was advanced by C. E. Shannon in a 1950 article in *Philosophical Magazine.* Since then, two schools of thought have emerged on the best way for computers to play chess.

One scheme is to have computers examine only a few lines of play, applying a large data base to the position at hand. The computer then makes a sophisticated generalization on the right course of action. This is how people usually play chess.

The other method, described as the brute-force approach, requires the computer to calculate deeply and swiftly into positions, mathematically evaluating moves in a thousand-per-second calculation. This is how computers generally do it because it's been programatically easier, and some computers thinking this way already play at an accomplished master level.

Each way has a disadvantage. It's hard to encode a computer with all the relevant information necessary for grand strategizing. Subtle features and tactics, of course, may be overlooked. The brute-force approach, on the other hand, picks up profound tactics, but does less well at grasping long-range plans and goals.

For years, theorists have tried to combine the best features of both methods, hoping to strike a balance between insightful evaluation and speedy calculation. The ultimate aim has been to achieve an effective parallel architecture, in which computers could perform both functions simultaneously. But in recent years the brute-force technique has needed little help, doing wonders on its own.

545 □ Will a computer ever be world champion?

Affirmative.

APPENDICES

PANDOLFINI'S SHORT CHESS COURSE

MOVES AND RULES

The Board: An 8 × 8 checkered board of 64 squares, 32 light and 32 dark.

Light Square Rule: Both players must have a light square in their near right corner.

Rows of Squares: Horizontal rows are ranks, vertical rows are files, and slanted rows are diagonals.

The Players: Two players. The lighter forces are called White, the darker Black.

The Forces: Each player starts with 16 units: 8 pieces (1 king, 1 queen, 2 rooks, 2 bishops, and 2 knights) and 8 pawns. Queens and rooks are major pieces, bishops and knights are minor pieces.

The Object: To checkmate the enemy king.

The First Move: White goes first, then Black, then White, etc.

A Move: Transfer of a unit from one square to another.

A Capture: Removal of an enemy unit from the board by moving to the square it occupies.

General Rules:	Move your own units. Capture your opponent's. Move 1 unit on a turn, except if castling. Move in 1 direction on a turn, except knights. Units move backward or forward, except pawns. Pawns move only forward. No move is compulsory unless it's the only legal one. The 6 kinds of units move in different ways. All, except pawns, capture the way they move. Only knights can jump over other units.
The King:	Moves 1 square in any direction.
The Rook:	Moves on ranks or files, as many unblocked squares as desired, one direction on a turn.
The Bishop:	Moves on diagonals of 1 color, as many unblocked squares as desired, one direction on a turn.
The Queen:	Moves like a rook or bishop, but only 1 direction on a turn.
The Knight:	Moves 1 square on a rank or file, then 2 at a right angle, or 2 on a rank or file, then 1 at a right angle. The complete move looks like the capital letter L. Always covers the same distance. Can jump over friendly and enemy units, as if nothing in way. From move to move, changes color of square occupied.
The Pawn:	Moves 1 square straight ahead. Each pawn has the option of advancing 2 squares on its first move. Captures 1 square diagonally ahead. Does not capture vertically.
Promotion:	Pawns reaching the last rank must be changed into a queen, rook, bishop or knight of the same color. No restrictions (you may have 2 or more queens).
En Passant:	Type of pawn capture. If a pawn is on its 5th rank, and an enemy pawn on an adjacent file advances 2 squares, the enemy pawn may be captured as if it had advanced only 1 square. The option may be exercised only on the first opportunity.
Check:	A direct attack to the king, a threat to capture it next move.
If "In Check":	A king must be taken out of check. It must be moved to safety, the check must be blocked (knight checks can't be blocked) or the checking unit must be captured.

Checkmate:

When a king can't be taken out of check, the game is over. The side giving check wins.

To Castle:

To move 2 pieces—the king and a rook—on the same turn. It must be the first move for both pieces. If the intervening squares are empty, move the king 2 spaces on the rank toward the rook and move the rook next to the king on the other side.

You Can't Castle:

If you are in check or castling into check, or if your king must pass over a square attacked by the enemy (cannot pass through check).

Draws:

There are 5 ways to draw: stalemate, agreement, 3-fold repetition, 50-move rule, and insufficient mating material.

Stalemate:

A player is stalemated if not in check but without a legal move.

Agreement:

One player offers a draw, the other accepts.

Repetition:

The player about to repeat the same position for the third time may claim a draw by indicating the intended repetition. The repetitions need not be on consecutive moves.

Fifty-Move Rule:

If 50 moves go by without a capture or pawn move, the player making the 50th move may claim a draw.

Insufficiency:

If neither player has enough material to mate, the game is drawn. For example, king vs. king.

Exchange Values:

A queen is worth about 9, a rook 5, a bishop 3, a knight 3, and a pawn 1.

Notation:

A way to write down chess moves. Pieces are abbreviated. King = K, queen = Q, rook = R, bishop = B, knight = N, pawn = P (if necessary). In algebraic notation, squares are named by combining a letter (for the file) and a number (for the rank). The files are lettered a–h, starting from White's left. The ranks are numbered 1–8, starting from White's side of the board. White's king starts on e1 and Black's on e8. Some other symbols: check = +, mate = + +, capture = ×, kingside castling = 0–0, queenside castling = 0–0–0, good move = !, bad move = ?. If both sides started by moving pawns in front of their kings 2 squares ahead, it's written: 1. e2–e4 e7–e5.

PRINCIPLES AND GUIDELINES

The Center

Play for it. Occupy, guard and influence it. Drive away enemy pieces that control it.

The Initiative

White, having the first move, starts with the initiative. Be aggressive. Don't waste time or moves. Try to attack in ways that build your game. Combine defense with counterattack. Don't be afraid to gambit a pawn for an opening attack, but don't sacrifice without sound reasons. Don't waste time capturing wing pawns at the expense of development.

Development

Use all pieces. Move only center pawns. Aim to develop a different piece on each turn. Move out minor pieces quickly. Castle early. Don't move the same piece repeatedly. Develop with threats.

Castling

Prepare to castle early in the game, especially if the center is open. Avoid weaknesses in front of the castled king. Castle for both defensive and offensive reasons (to safeguard the king and to activate a rook).

Pawns

Move both center pawns, one or two squares ahead, preferably two. Make few pawn moves. Bad pawn moves create weak squares. Don't block center pawns by moving bishops in front of them. Don't move pawns in front of the castled king's position. Trade pawns to avoid loss of material, open lines, or save time.

Knights

Develop knights toward the center. The White to f3 and c3, the Black to c6 and f6. Develop them elsewhere only if needed or for a particular purpose (e.g. move the KN to h3 to guard f2). Generally, move at least one knight before any bishops. Avoid getting knights pinned diagonally by bishops to the king or queen, and on the e-file by rooks to the king.

Bishops

Place them on open diagonals. Use them to guard center squares, pin enemy knights or defensively to break pins. Flank them if part of a plan to control squares of one color. Avoid unnecessary exchanges for knights. Use them to back up queen and knight attacks.

Rooks

Put them on open files (clear of all pawns), half-open files (clear of friendly pawns) or behind advanced friendly pawns. Double them, so that they support each other. Sometimes develop them by moving the pawn in front. Use them to attack the uncastled enemy king along the e-file and to pin enemy units. If feasible, place them on the 7th rank.

The Queen

Don't move it too early. Don't move it too much. Avoid developing it where it can be attacked. Don't use it if weaker units would suffice. Use it to set up multiple attacks, alone or in combination with other forces. Don't be afraid to trade it for the enemy queen if desirable or to avoid difficulties.

Analysis

Evaluate the major elements: material, pawn structure, time, space, and king safety. Elicit information about the position with probing questions. For example: Why did she do that? Did he respond to my last move satisfactorily? Etc.

Planning

Plan early. Don't change plans without good reason. But be flexible. Modify your plan if desirable or necessary. Base your plan on an analysis of the position, noting strengths and weaknesses, and accounting for definite threats.

The Endgame

Threaten to make new queens by advancing passed pawns. Force your opponent to surrender material trying to stop you. Activate the king. Trade pieces, not pawns, when ahead in material. Position rooks actively behind enemy pawns. Place them on the 7th rank. Don't tie them down to defense. With an extra queen, try to force mate.

MIDDLEGAME STRATEGIES

Enemy Problem	Do This Against It
1. Bad minor piece:	avoid its exchange; keep it restricted.
2. Blocked pieces:	keep them blocked.
3. Cramped game:	avoid freeing exchanges.
4. Down the exchange:	simplify to ending of rook vs. minor piece; invade with **K & R**, produce passed pawn.
5. Exposed king:	threaten with pieces; look for double attacks.
6. Ill-timed flank attack:	counter in the center.
7. Lack of development:	look for tactics and combinations.
8. Unprotected pieces:	look for forks.
9. Material disadvantage:	trade pieces, not pawns.
10. Moved pawns around castled king:	attack with pieces in open positions; pawn storm in closed positions; generally, occupy weakened squares.
11. Overextended pawns:	undermine with pawns, attack with pieces.
12. Pawn-grabbing:	develop and attack the king.
13. Pinned units:	pile up on them; attack with pawns and lesser units.

14. Premature queen moves:	attack it with development.
15. Time trouble:	make good, surprise threats.
16. Uncastled king:	prevent castling; open the center.
17. Under heavy attack:	shun simplification until you gain something.
18. Unfavorable majorities:	advance healthy majority; create passed pawn.
19. Weak pawns:	fix and exploit and attack.
20. Weak squares:	occupy them.

ENDGAME: PRINCIPLES AND ADVICE

1. Familiarize yourself with the endgames likely to stem from the openings you play.

2. Exploit advantages and minimize disadvantages. That's the plan.

3. Be dynamic.

4. Don't play aimlessly. Don't waste moves. Don't give pointless checks.

5. Deploy all pieces. Activate the king.

6. Cut off lines and cut down enemy threats. Restrain your opponent.

7. If winning, intensify your efforts. It can be hard to win a won game.

8. If losing, look for positional draws, fortresses, stalemates, and sucker punches.

9. Inflict multiple weaknesses on your opponent, preferably in different sectors, and set up winning double threats.

10. Avoid weakening pawn moves.

11. If you have weaknesses, liquidate them.

12. If an enemy pawn is weak, don't trade it. Win it.

13. Create a passed pawn. Use it.

14. Don't be precipitate. If a pawn is attackable, be able to defend it. Ready the king.

15. Don't hurry, but if there's a race, win it.

16. Escort passed pawns. The king clears the way.

17. If the king can't get in front, get behind. Get somewhere.

18. If the king can't blockade, block out.

19. *Zugzwang* your opponent. Achieve meaningful oppositions.

20. When mobilizing a majority, push the unopposed pawn first.

21. If stalled, open a second front. Create another passed pawn. Decoy your opponent.

22. Don't make too many extra queens. Two queens are enough.

23. If ahead by a pawn, exchange pieces, not pawns. If behind by a pawn, exchange pawns, not pieces.

24. Avoid getting stuck with rook-pawns, unless it's a special case.

25. Corral. Bishops should restrict knights.

26. Opposite-color bishops: blockade to draw, create passed pawns to win.

27. Anchor the good knight.

28. Don't put pawns on the same color as your bishop.

29. Fix pawns to impede the enemy bishop.

30. With two bishops, swap one to get a winning minor piece ending.

31. Weaponize rooks. To insure activity, you may have to sac a pawn or two.

32. Rook-attack from far away. Seek the "checking distance."

33. Put rooks behind passed pawns. If not, flank attack.

34. In rook endings, if your king must bail out, flee to the short side of the enemy pawn. Keep the long side for your rook.

35. Shelter your king from pesky rooks. If necessary, build a bridge.

36. Blockade with the king, not the rook.

37. In pure queen endings, centralize your queen, choke the enemy's.

38. Eschew greed. Cede extra material if it eases the win.

39. Trade to simplify, shun to keep complex. If winning, clarify; if losing, complicate.

40. Play like Lasker and burn this list.

TIPS FOR THE NATIONALS AND OTHER TOURNAMENTS

1. If you have White, think before you play your first move.

2. If you have Black, think before your opponent's first move.

3. If you have White, after Black's first move, think of a development scheme. Before playing your second move, determine how to develop the minor pieces and which pawns to move. Consider the safety of your king and the placement of the rooks and queen.

4. Take at least a couple of minutes to do this.

5. Don't play automatic moves. Make sure you understand the opening before playing it.

6. If your opponent plays an unusual move, try to understand it before responding. Answer all threats.

7. Make as few pawn moves as necessary.

8. Select a plan and stay with it. Don't switch without good reason.

9. Concentrate. Keep your attention on the board. Don't let your mind wander, and don't you wander either. Don't get up from the board unless you must.

10. Use your time to find the best move and your opponent's time to think of future possibilities.

11. Whenever possible, attack. If you must defend, try to do it while also counterattacking.

12. Record the game very carefully, especially the first ten moves. Write each move immediately before or after it's played. Do not play several moves and then record, even on forced responses.

13. Always call touch move. If it's called on you, put the piece back on its original square and consider your options. Do not hold the piece in your hand while thinking.

14. Play to win in as few moves as necessary. Don't waste time gobbling your opponent's pawns when you're well ahead. Go for the jugular. Play for mate.

15. If you blunder, don't resign. Sit back and figure out how to give your opponent trouble. Go down fighting and you might live to fight again.

16. If ahead, exchange pieces. If behind, avoid piece trades.

17. If ahead, avoid pawn trades unless the position calls for it. If behind, trade pawns unless there's a problem.

18. If cramped, try to free your game by exchanges. If your opponent is cramped, keep it that way.

19. If under attack, swap off some of the attackers. If attacking, avoid needless exchanges.

20. Don't go pawn-grabbing.

21. If your king is still in the middle, don't open the center. If your king is castled and your opponent's isn't, open the center.

22. Prevent the enemy from castling. Don't sacrifice a piece to stop enemy castling without concrete follow-up. A pawn is something else. Sac one if your chances seem reasonable.

23. If your opponent attacks on the flank, counter in the center.

24. In most cases, attack with pieces, not pawns.

25. Seize open lines. Reinforce and exploit them.

26. Grab a key open file first. With a rook on the file, occupy an anchor point (a safe square on the same file supported by at least one pawn). Be alert to rook lifts, shifting a rook to the other wing. If you can, double rooks. If you need, triple major pieces.

27. Neutralize enemy rooks. Oppose them. If this is wrong, take another file, or open your own. Don't exchange rooks if it surrenders the file.

28. Get a "pig" (occupy the 7th rank with a rook). If defending against a rook on the 7th, don't advance pawns that elongate the rook's control of the 7th (don't lengthen the pig). If your rook is attacking on the 7th,

reinforce it by doubling rooks (strengthen the pig). Place two rooks on the 7th and open a sty.

29. Don't move the pawns in front of your castled king without good reason.

30. Turn weaknesses into strengths. For example, if your castled king is exposed to attack along a half-open g-file, move the king to the corner and put a rook on the g-file. Make your opponent sweat.

31. Accept all sacrifices you don't understand. Don't sacrifice without good reason. Try to sacrifice your opponent's pieces.

32. Don't play the first good move that comes into your head. Open your eyes and you might find a better one.

33. If your opponent is in time pressure, don't rush your moves. Take some time to find surprising moves that force your opponent to think.

34. In the endgame, make good use of your king. Keep your rooks active. They work best from far away. Don't let your rooks idle in defense. Try to create a meaningful passed pawn. Convoy it home. Don't make lots of extra queens. One will do. Otherwise, you increase the chance for stalemate. With an extra queen, mate as soon as possible. If lost, find a stalemate shot or set up a fortress.

35. Don't play a move you know to be unsound unless you're busted. In that case, you have nothing to lose, so look for a sucker punch.

36. Don't be frightened by higher-rated opponents. They have more to lose than you do. Have some fun. Go for the kill.

37. Take no prisoners. Draw only if you must. If offered a draw, make sure you understand what it means to accept it.

38. Be serious. Don't talk to your opponent during the game. If he or she talks to you, complain. You can be chummy after the game, not during it.

39. Chess is a creative process. Its purpose is to find the truth. To discover the truth, you must be uncompromising. You must be brave.

40. Play as if the future of humanity depends on your efforts. It does.

TIPS FOR THE NATIONALS AND OTHER TOURNAMENTS

LEVEL TWO

---

1. **Touch Move.** If you touch a piece and your opponent calls you on it, don't move it right away. Put the piece back on its starting square and find the best move for it. Don't keep the piece in your hand while you're thinking. That cuts down on your vision of the board. Enforce the touch move rule against everyone.

2. **Draw Offers.** Don't accept or propose a draw in the last two rounds without understanding what it means. It could hurt your team's standing, as well as your own. Generally, don't take or offer a draw unless you're dead lost or feeling very sick.

3. **Concentration.** Focus on the game in front of you, not the one next to you. Don't get up from the board without a good reason. Don't talk to your opponent during the game. If he or she talks to you, complain to a tournament director. To achieve perfect concentration, be prepared to stick your fingers in your ears. All sound must be blotted out. Good concentration is the secret to winning chess.

4. **Recording.** Record each game carefully. The only exception is when you are in time trouble. In that case, try to check off each move played. Write down each half move immediately before or after playing it. Make sure to record your opponent's move before responding, even on obvious plays. If you don't, it means you're moving too quickly. This could result in an unbalanced score sheet, and you could become terribly confused. You might try writing down your moves before playing them. This may enable you to catch a mistake before making it. Sometimes your opponent reacts to the written move and tips you off. If your opponent becomes tense and very still, for example, he or she might be trying to conceal something, hoping you don't realize your move is an error. Exploit this. Moreover, in straining to read your

scoresheet, your opponent's attention may be diverted from the board itself, and that could prove costly—to your opponent.

5. **The Opening.** Don't play the opening casually, no matter how well you think you know it. Make sure you understand what's going on. If your opponent plays a strange-looking move, take some time to analyze it. Fight for the initiative right from the start. Especially in an evening round, try to win efficiently so you can go to sleep. (This doesn't mean you should move quickly.)

6. **Between Rounds.** Play no chess between rounds. It will sap you. Get some exercise instead. And please: no junk food.

7. **Blunders.** If you blunder, don't immediately resign, and don't play as if you're going to lose. Fight on as if it's the Crimean War. If you blunder, don't respond quickly. The second blunder might kill you. Instead of aimless moving, as if the game is hopelessly lost, take a few minutes to evaluate the position. Try to get your head back into the game. Figure out a strategy to maximize your chances. There's always a best course of action, even when lost. Make sure you find it.

8. **Strategies when Losing.** If you're behind by a pawn, don't trade pieces; trade pawns. If it comes down to a minor piece and a pawn vs. a minor piece, you may be able to sacrifice the piece to draw the game. (If you're ahead, trade pieces, not pawns.) Avoid the endgame unless you can achieve a positional draw. You can trade, for instance, to reach an endgame with bishops of opposite colors. Such endings often draw, even if one player is ahead by a few pawns. You also can exchange if you can saddle your opponent with a rook-pawn and a bishop that doesn't control the rook-pawn's promotion square. Look for such fortresses. In general, fight on tooth and nail. Make your opponent earn the point. No one ever won by resigning.

9. **Sucker Punches.** If you're really busted, look for sucker punches. A sucker punch is a double threat, where one of the threats is obvious and the other is subtle. Your opponent might fixate on the obvious one and overlook the subtle one. Especially try to find mating shots, the more the better. When you're dead lost you can take chances because you have nothing to lose.

10. **Materially Behind.** If you're materially behind, complicate the position. Avoid simplifying moves and exchanges. (If you're ahead, ruthlessly simplify.) Exchange only if you can force a known drawn ending. If you are materially ahead, and if under attack, don't be afraid to give back some of your material to break your opponent's attack. If material is even and you are under attack, swap off a few pieces to lessen your opponent's threats. If cramped, look to exchange to free your game. The fewer pieces you have, the less cramped you are.

11. **Enemy Sacrifices.** If your opponent offers a sacrifice, accept it

unless you can see clearly that it would be bad to do so. A pawn is a pawn in any country in the world. Punish mistakes without mercy.

12. Defense. The best defense is a good offense. Look for counterattacks. If you must defend, try to combine protection with counterplay, making sure to reply to all enemy threats. Issue threats of your own to seize the initiative. The best way to upset your opponent's plans is to become menacing.

13. King in the Center. If your opponent is castled, don't open the center when your own king is still in the middle. That's the surest way to get mated quickly. If kings are castled, counter a flank attack by playing in the center. If kings are castled on opposite sides, move the pawns in front of the enemy king to open lines of attack. The best way to stop an enemy threat to your king is to attack your opponent's.

14. Pawn-grabbing. Don't go pawn-grabbing in the opening, especially if it involves overuse of the queen. It could cost you several moves. Instead of taking risky pawns, develop quickly and play for mate.

15. Pawn Moves. Make as few pawn moves as necessary. Pawn moves tend to create weaknesses (squares that can't be guarded by pawns). Especially avoid them around your castled king's position. When attacking, particularly in open positions, use pieces. If you don't know what to do, make an intelligent piece move. Unless there is a specific need or reason, make pawn moves only to facilitate development in the opening, open lines for attack in the middlegame, or create passed pawns in the endgame.

16. Endgames. As soon as you get to the endgame, activate the king. Bring it back to the center or somewhere useful. If there are rooks on the board, please make sure to avoid back-rank mates by making *luft* or centralizing the king. Try to create a passed pawn and make a queen. Keep your pieces active. Rooks are effective from far away. Don't place your pawns on the same color as your bishop. Bishops tend to be better than knights. In king-and-pawn endings, try to clear paths for your pawns with your king. Remember the value of diagonal king moves. With them, you can often cover more territory and accomplish multiple aims. Don't waste time making lots of queens. Once you get an extra queen, force mate. Win as soon as possible.

17. Minor Pieces. Choose your minor pieces wisely. In open games, prefer bishops. In horribly blocked-up games, keep at least one knight. If you have a bishop, place your pawns on squares of the opposite color. Try to anchor your knights on strong central squares. With bishops of opposite colors, the attacker has the advantage in the middlegame because the enemy bishop can't neutralize the opposing bishop. Endgames with opposite-color bishops are often drawn. For attacking purposes, a queen and knight are often stronger than a queen and bishop, especially if the knight offers the queen more support points (being able to guard squares of both colors), and when the action takes place mainly on one side of the board.

18. **The Clock.** If you're playing with a clock, record how much time you have used after move five, move ten, move fifteen, and move twenty (unless you find this too distracting). These signposts can be helpful to you and your coach. The best way to beat an opponent in time trouble is not to rush your own moves. Instead, think a bit and look for strong, unexpected moves that require your opponent to use up time on the clock.

19. **Your Move—Your Opponent's Move.** On your move, be specific. Try to find the best answer to your opponent's previous play. If you can, issue threats of your own. When it's your opponent's turn, think generally. Ask those questions you didn't have time to ask on your own move. Which side would you like to castle on? Where would you like to place various pieces? Where are your opponent's potential targets? And so on. Be particular on your move, and general on your opponent's move. Make sure to use your opponent's time productively.

20. **Planning.** Be flexible, but settle on a plan and stay with it. Don't change it without good reason. But don't be too rigid either. Change your plans if you can thereby gain advantage.

Go Out and Conquer the World!

GLOSSARY

Activate: To develop, improve the position of, mobilize, or make more aggressive.

Active: Aggressive, with regard to a move, variation, or placement.

Advantage: Superiority in development, space, material, pawn structure, or king safety, or in any combination of these.

Analysis: The process of determining through careful examination the best moves in a variation or position.

Attack: (*n*) A threat to capture an enemy unit. A force aimed at a specific objective or for a definite purpose. (*v*) To make moves or a series of moves to mate, gain material, or obtain advantage.

Back Rank: The rank occupied by all eight enemy pieces in the original position.

Back-Rank Mate: A mate given by a queen or rook along the board's edge. Also called a back-row mate.

Backward Pawn: A pawn whose neighboring pawns are too far advanced to protect it. Usually a weakness, generally restrained by enemy units, often subject to frontal attack along the file it occupies.

Base of the Pawn Chain: When two or more pawns for each side block and immobilize their enemy counterparts, the base is the pawn closest to its own home rank (for each side).

Bad Bishop: A passive bishop, often obstructed by its own pawns; usually a permanent disadvantage.

Basic Mate: A checkmate that can be forced against a lone king by any of four different combinations: a king and a queen, a king and a rook, a king and two bishops, or a king, a bishop, and a knight.

Battery: Two or more pieces of like power attacking supportively along the same line.

Bind: A grip, usually held by pawns, preventing the enemy from relieving a cramped game.

Bishop Pair: The advantage of having two bishops against a bishop and a knight or two knights. See *two bishops* and *two-bishop advantage*.

Bishops of Opposite Color: A situation in which each player has only one bishop, one traveling on light squares, the other on dark.

Blockade: A defensive strategy aimed at preventing the advance of an enemy pawn, especially a passed pawn, by stationing a piece directly in front of it and guarding that square with other pieces and pawns.

Blunder: A meaningful error.

Book Move: A viable opening move appearing in current chess literature.

Breakthrough: Usually a pawn move (or moves) to clear lines and penetrate enemy terrain, often by means of a sacrifice.

Building a Bridge: In rook endings, a technique to create shelter for a king and/or a passed pawn.

Candidate: A pawn likely to become passed. A pawn with no enemy pawn in front of it on the same file. Also called a candidate passed pawn.

Capablanca's Rule: When mobilizing a pawn majority, start by moving the unopposed pawn.

Center: The four squares, e4, d4, d5, e5, taken as a block. Loosely, the surrounding squares as well.

Centralization: Moving pieces towards the center.

Checking Distance: The minimum distance a rook needs to attack without being in danger of counterattack by an approaching enemy king. It's especially important in the endgame.

Chessmen: A sexist term to describe the material figures. Use "units" or "pieces and pawns."

Classical: A school or style of play that favors direct occupation of the center and a systematic, often dogmatic approach to strategy.

Clearance: Evacuating a square or line, often by sacrifice, so that another friendly unit can occupy or exploit the same square or line.

Classical Pawn Center: Two White pawns, on d4 and e4; or two Black pawns, on d5 and e5.

Closed Center: A center blocked by both sides' pawns and therefore impassable to pieces.

Closed File: A file containing pawns for both players, so neither side's queens or rooks can move all the way through it.

Closed Game: One in which the center is blocked by pawns, in which few, if any, exchanges have taken place.

Combination: A forced series of moves, usually involving sacrifice, always leading to an improvement of one's situation.

Compensation: A counterbalancing advantage.

Connected: For pieces, occupying the same line and capable of supporting each other (connected rooks); for pawns, occupying adjacent files and capable of defending each other.

Connected Passed Pawns: Two friendly passed pawns on adjacent files, usually occupying the same or a nearby rank.

Consolidate: To stabilize a loose or uncoordinated position, often by playing several defensive or simplifying moves (exchanging pieces), temporarily abandoning the immediate attack.

Corral: The trapping of a knight by a bishop along the edge.

Corresponding Square: In endgame theory, a square that corresponds to an enemy square in a complex oppositional relationship distorted by fixed groups of White and Black pawns. Usually appearing in White and Black pairs, they are often referred to in the plural as "corresponding squares." Like land mines, both kings avoid stepping on them first.

Counterattack: An attack mounted by the defender or a player who is apparently defending.

Cramped: Blocked by pawns, usually on the third rank; constricted.

Critical Square: One whose occupation by the superior king insures completing a task.

Cross Check: A check that blocks the enemy's previous check.

Cut-off: A queen, rook, or bishop barrier that the enemy king can't cross.

Decoy: An outside passed pawn offered as a sacrifice to lure an enemy piece (usually the king) out of position.

Deflection: Forcing an enemy unit from its post, leaving a certain square or set of squares inadequately guarded.

Development: Moving a piece to a better square, or improving its scope or potential by moving a pawn out of its way.

Discovery: Moving a unit and thereby unveiling an attack by another friendly unit, often resulting in two attacks simultaneously; one from the moving unit and one from the stationary one. Also called a discovered attack.

Double Attack: Two or more threats stemming from the same move.

Double Check: Two checks given by the same move; a discovery in which both the moving and stationary units give check.

Doubled Pawns: Two friendly pawns occupying the same file.

Down the Exchange: Having a knight or bishop against an enemy rook.

Edge: Any of the board's four outside rows: the a-file, the eighth rank, the h-file, or the first rank.

Elements: The factors that determine which side has the advantage. There are many elements, but the five basic ones are space, time, pawn structure, material, and king safety.

Endgame: The third and final phase of a chess game, after the opening and middlegame.

En Prise: "In take." A French term designating an unprotected unit subject to capture.

Exchange: (*n*) An equal trade. Also, *the exchange:* The loss or gain of a rook for a minor piece, as in "win *the* exchange." (*v*) To trade equal amounts of material.

Exchange Values: The relative values of the pieces and pawns: a pawn is worth one, a bishop or knight three, a rook five, and a queen nine.

Family Fork: A triple knight fork to the enemy king, queen, and rook. Also called a royal fork.

Fianchetto: A flank development of a bishop, usually to a knight-two square.

Fixed: Blocked, or held in place.

Fixed Center: A center containing a pair of fixed pawns.

Fixed Pawns: Two pawns, one White and one Black, facing and blocking each other along the same file, so that neither can move.

Flank: Usually, the two outer rows on either side of the board, though sometimes including the adjacent bishop file.

Flank Openings: An opening in which White doesn't necessarily occupy the center with pawns, instead relying on off-center advances and opting to fianchetto at least one bishop.

Force: (*n*) General term for material. (*v*) To limit enemy responses to a single legal or practical move.

Fork: A tactic by which a friendly unit attacks at least two enemy units with the same move.

Fork Trick: A combination that wins a pawn or trades center pawns favorably. A piece is temporarily sacrificed and regained by a subsequent pawn fork.

Fortress: In the endgame, a situation in which an inferior force can prevent a superior force from realizing its advantage by setting up a defensive wall or barrier.

Frontier: The imaginary line dividing the board in half horizontally.

Gaining a Move: Creating the same position but with the other player to move, completing a sequence in one less move than expected, or forcing your opponent to waste a move.

Gambit: A voluntary sacrifice in the opening, usually of a pawn, offered to build the initiative or the attack, or to blunt your opponent's initiative or attack.

Good Bishop: A bishop unimpeded by its own pawns, usually opposing a bad bishop that is so blocked.

Grandmaster Draw: A lifeless draw in the opening or early middle-game.

Half-Open File: A file, occupied by only one pawn, that the other side's major pieces can use for attack.

Hanging: Simultaneously attacked and unprotected. A related term is *en prise*.

Hanging Pawns: Adjacent friendly pawns, occupying the same rank, usually subject to attack, but sometimes capable of advancing with advantage.

Heavy Piece: A major piece; either a queen or rook.

Hole: A weakness, usually a square on one's third rank, incapable of being defended by a pawn and therefore ideal for occupation by enemy pieces.

Hypermodern: A school or style advocating several ideas opposed to classical principles, such as controlling the center initially from the flank rather than directly occupying it.

In-Between Move: A move that interrupts an apparently forced sequence. A finesse that gains time or some other advantage. Also called a *zwischenzug*.

Indirect Defense: Defending a unit without actually guarding it, by tactically or practically preventing its capture.

Initiative: The ability to attack and force the play.

Isolated Pawn: A pawn with no friendly pawns on adjacent files and therefore incapable of being defended by a pawn. Generally, a weakness.

Isolani: Nimzovich's term for the isolated queen-pawn, which can be a weakness or a strength, depending on circumstances. Often signifying any isolated pawn.

King Safety: One of the five main elements of chess, along with time, space, pawn structure, and material.

Knight's Corral: A bishop trap of a knight on the edge.

Knight's Jump: A measure of distance based on the length and shape of a knight's move. If a unit is a knight's jump away from a knight, it's in position to be captured by the knight (if circumstances permit).

Line: A rank, file, or diagonal.

Long Side: The side of a pawn offering the greatest number of files to the edge of the board. See "short side."

Lose a Move: Create *zugzwang* by transferring the same position to the other player, making it your opponent's turn to move.

Losing the Exchange: Losing a rook for a minor piece.

Luft: an escape square for the king. When you move a pawn to create an escape square, you "make *luft*."

Major Piece: A queen or rook.

Man: A shortened version of the sexist term "chessmen."

Maneuver: (*n*) The repositioning of a piece. (*v*) To transfer a piece in two or more moves.

Material: Pieces and pawns collectively.

Mating Material: Sufficient material to force mate.

Middlegame: The second phase of a chess game, after the opening and before the endgame.

Minor Exchange: A term signifying the slight material edge a bishop has over a knight. You "win the minor exchange" if you gain a bishop for a knight.

Minor Pieces: Bishops and knights.

Minority Attack: An attack by several pawns against a larger group of pawns.

Mobility: Freedom of movement. The number of squares available to a piece.

Notation: A system to record chess moves. If you keep notation, you write down the moves of the game.

Open Center: A center unblocked by pawns, through which pieces can move.

Open File: A file without pawns on it. Sometimes, a half-open file is loosely called an open file for the player able to use it.

Open Game: A game in which at least a pair of center pawns have been exchanged, so that movement through the center is possible. Most open games, though not all, stem from king-pawn openings.

Opening: The beginning phase of a chess game, usually lasting 10 or 15 moves.

Open Line: A rank, file, or diagonal unobstructed by pawns.

Opposite-Color Bishops: See *bishops of opposite colors.*

Opposition: In endgames, a *zugzwang* relationship between the opposing kings, in which it's advantageous not to be on the move.

Outflanking: In the endgame, a general invasion from the flank by one king against the other, often against fixed pawn formations, designed to win a pawn.

Outpost: A weak square, incapable of being guarded by enemy pawns, supported by at least one friendly pawn, usually on the enemy's third or fourth rank, that can be occupied by a piece to good effect. The defender's hole is the attacker's outpost.

Outside Critical Square: In any set of three critical squares, the one farthest from the enemy king.

Outside Passed Pawn: The passed pawn farthest from the main fighting area or from the two kings, often used as a decoy.

Overload: A tactic exploiting an overburdened piece's inability to fulfill all its defensive commitments.

Overworked Piece: An overloaded piece, unable to honor its protective commitments.

Passed Pawn: A pawn capable of advancing to promotion because no enemy pawns can block it or guard squares in its path.

Passive: Refers to a move that merely guards, wards off threats, or marks time, as opposed to an active attacking or counterattacking move.

Pawn Chain: An interlocking group of friendly and enemy pawns blocking each other's movement. White's pawns form one obstructive diagonal (or chain), while Black's occupy another impeding diagonal (or chain). Loosely, any diagonal series of friendly pawns.

Pawn-grabbing: Taking risky pawns at the expense of development and position.

Pawn Island: A group of pawns separated from other friendly pawns by at least one file. A pawn island may contain one or more pawns.

Pawn Majority: A troop of friendly pawns outnumbering enemy pawns over the same number of files.

Pawn Structure: The overall configuration of pawns. One of the five elements of chess.

Pawn Weakness: A pawn that can be exploited or that can't be defended adequately by other friendly pawns.

Permanent Advantage: A lasting advantage, such as material or pawn structure. The opposite is a *temporary advantage*.

Pig: Chess jargon for a rook on the seventh rank.

Pin: A tactic preventing or dissuading an enemy unit from moving off a line for fear of exposing a friendly unit to capture or a key square to occupation. The pinned unit is in the unenviable situation of being a shield.

Positional Draw: A draw agreed to for practical reasons; a position that should be a draw. Though the attacker has enough material to win, mate can't be forced and the defender can prevent progress.

Principle: A general truth, often a maxim, frequently expressed as a "do" or a "don't," serving as a guide for reasonable play.

Problem Bishop: A bishop generally blocked by its own pawns, resulting from a specific opening.

Protected Passed Pawn: A passed pawn defended by another pawn and generally safe from capture by enemy pieces.

Pseudo Sacrifice: An apparent sacrifice that can't be accepted without incurring disadvantage. Often, merely a step in a forced winning combination. Also called a sham sacrifice.

Queening: Promoting a pawn to a queen.

Queenside Majority: An advantage in pawns on the queenside often leading to the creation of an outside passed pawn (a decoy). Also called a queenside pawn majority.

Real Sacrifice: The opposite of a pseudo or sham sacrifice; a material sacrifice involving risk, in that its consequences can't be seen precisely. Also called a *true sacrifice.*

Removing the Defender: A tactic making a unit vulnerable by capturing, luring or driving away, or immobilizing its protector. Also called removing the guard or undermining.

Sacrifice: A voluntary surrender of material for attack or positional advantages.

Seventh Rank: The ideal rank for a rook to occupy. A rook on the seventh rank often attacks a row of enemy pawns, confines the enemy king, and generally attacks and issues powerful threats.

Sham Sacrifice: A sacrifice in name only, for its consequences are known and clearly favorable. Also called a *pseudo sacrifice.*

Short Side: The side of a pawn with the fewest number of files to the edge. The side with the most files to the edge is the long side. Every pawn, except the rook-pawn, has a long and short side.

Simplification: Exchanging pieces to avoid complications, clarifying an advantage.

Skewer: The opposite of a pin. A straight-line tactic in which an enemy piece is compelled to move off the line of attack, exposing on the same line another unit to capture or a key square to occupation.

Space: One of the five main elements of chess, generally based on mobility and the number of squares influenced and controlled.

Square of the Pawn: A trick to determine if a king can overtake a passed pawn by visualizing if the pawn fits inside an imagined quadrangle.

Squeeze: An endgame *zugzwang*, in which a pawn move to the seventh rank, without giving check, forces the defending king to leave the back rank so that the attacking king can advance, seizing control of the promotion square.

Strategy: General, long-term planning, as opposed to specific, immediate actions (tactics).

Support Mate: A checkmate given by a protected queen on a square adjacent to the enemy king.

Swindle: A trap that wins or draws an otherwise lost game (if the opponent falls for it).

Symmetrical Opening: An opening in which both White and Black play essentially the same moves, though not necessarily in the same order. At some point, the player with the initiative, usually White, will break the symmetry by playing a move that can't be copied.

System: A set of related opening variations branching from a particular move or group of moves, in which pieces and pawns are positioned for harmonious purposes, with corresponding logic, and in which definite middlegame plans emerge.

Tactics: Short-term, immediate attacks and threats.

Tempo: A unit of chess time. The time represented by a move. Plural: tempi.

Temporary Advantage: A fleeting advantage, such as space, time, or king safety, that must be exploited quickly or it evaporates. The opposite is a *permanent advantage*.

Threat: A direct or indirect attack, which must be answered.

Time: One of the main elements of chess, usually evaluated in terms of initiative and development.

Touch Move: A rule requiring the player to move the first unit touched on the player's turn.

Trade: (*n*) An exchange of equal material. (*v*) To make such a transaction.

Transpose: In a variation, to reverse or change the order of moves to arrive at the same position.

Trap: A baited variation to lure a careless opponent into error.

Trapped Piece: A threatened piece that can't escape attack, and therefore is lost.

Triangulation: In endgames, a maneuver by which a king (rarely a queen) takes two moves to occupy a square it could have reached in one. It's usually done to lose a move, placing the other side in *zugzwang*.

True Sacrifice: Another name for *real sacrifice*.

Two Bishops: A type of advantage in which one side has two bishops while the other has a bishop and knight or two knights. Also referred to as the *bishop pair* or the *two-bishop advantage*.

Two-Bishop Advantage: See *two bishops* and *bishop pair*.

Undermining: See *removing the defender*.

Underpromotion: Promoting a pawn to either a rook, a bishop, or a knight, but not a queen.

Up the Exchange: Having the advantage of a rook against a minor piece.

Variation: A sequence of moves, particularly in the opening.

Waiting Move: A move that shifts the turn to the opponent without changing anything important in the position.

Weakness: A square inadequately defended, generally not capable of being guarded by pawns. The term also refers to any tactical vulnerability.

Winning the Exchange: Gaining a rook for a minor piece.

X-ray: A skewer attack or defense.

Zugzwang: A German word meaning "compulsion to move." In the endgame, you are "in *zugzwang*" when any move you make worsens your situation. At other times, the word simply means having no useful move.

Zwischenzug: A German word meaning "intermediate move." Also called "in-between move." Usually it's a way to gain an advantage by playing an unexpected finesse, which delays an obvious response, such as a recapture.

INDEX

About the Author

BRUCE PANDOLFINI is the author of fourteen instructional chess books, including *Chessercizes; More Chessercizes: Checkmate; Bobby Fischer's Outrageous Chess Moves; Principles of the New Chess; Pandolfini's Endgame Course; Russian Chess; The ABC's of Chess; Let's Play Chess; Kasparov's Winning Chess Tactics; One-Move Chess by the Champions; Chess Openings: Traps and Zaps; Square One; and Weapons of Chess.* He is also the editor of the distinguished anthologies *The Best of Chess Life & Review,* Volumes I and II, and has produced, with David MacEnulty, two instructional videotapes, *Understanding Chess* and *Opening Principles.*

Bruce was the chief commentator at the New York half of the 1990 Kasparov–Karpov World Chess Championship, and in 1990 was head coach of the United States Team in the World Youth Chess Championships in Wisconsin. Perhaps the most experienced chess teacher in North America, he is the co-founder, with Faneuil Adams, of the Manhattan Chess Club School, and is the director of the New York City Schools Program. Bruce's most famous student, six-time National Scholastic Champion Joshua Waitzkin, is the subject of Fred Waitzkin's acclaimed book *Searching for Bobby Fischer.* Bruce Pandolfini lives in Manhattan.